The Ultimate Guide to WEIGHT TRAINING for RUNNING

second edition

Prior to beginning any exercise program, you must consult with your physician. You must also consult your physician before increasing the intensity of your training.

Any application of the recommended material in this book is at the sole risk of the reader, and at the readers discretion. Responsibility of any injuries or other negative effects resulting from the application of any of the information provided within this book is expressly disclaimed.

Published by Price World Enterprises
28550 Belcourt Rd
Pepper Pike, OH 44124

Book layout and typesetting by Just Your Type DTP
Cover design by Alexandru Dan Georgescu
Interior photographs by Marc Gollub
Editing by Barb Greenberg
Editing and proofreading by Maryanne Haselow-Dulin
Printing by RJ Communications

Second Edition, 2005
ISBN: 1-932549-43-9

Printed in the United States of America
10 9 8 7 6 5 4 3 2

Special thanks to:
Dr. Marc B. Price CPFT for your expert insight and helpful contributions
Zack, David, and Gail Price for your support and encouragement to make this book possible.

The Ultimate Guide to WEIGHT TRAINING for RUNNING

second edition

sportsworkout.com

CONTENTS

Part I

Running Specific Training

With Weight Training, Knowledge is the Key to Success

INTRODUCTION

By opening *The Ultimate Guide to Weight Training for Running,* you have taken your first step towards achieving your athletic potential. This book is loaded with the most up-to-date sports weight training information and features a year-round running-specific weight-training program. Upon completion of the text, you will know how to properly, safely, and effectively perform over 80 exercises and you will be ready to begin your training.

The true importance of this book lies in the running-specific program in the front of the book. It was created for one reason and one reason only: to improve your running potential. It does this by increasing your strength, endurance, and flexibility in the parts of your body that are most important for running. The program was designed to supply you with the advantage you will need to outperform your opponents. By following the program, you will build your muscles with endurance and stamina. When called upon, you will be physically prepared and mentally ready to compete at the highest of your potential.

Although running is primarily a sport focusing on leg strength and endurance, certain upper-body muscle groups should not be ignored in order to achieve your maximum potential. *The Ultimate Guide to Weight Training for Running* does not overlook the importance of these muscle groups and has you training your entire body in order to maximize your potential.

This book does not teach you how to perform specific movements. It does not show you the best strategies to perfect your running technique, nor does it give you any tips to improve your specific running skills. This book does, however, provide you with the best methods, programs, and strategies available to physically improve your body and maximize your running potential!

Before you begin every weight-training session, this book recommends that you perform at least five minutes of abdominal work to warm yourself up and to train your midsection.

If you are really serious about training for running you should strongly consider subscribing to our online Sport-Specific e-Training Program where you will be matched up with one of our online sport-specific trainers for one on one training and consultation. Your trainer will create personalized training programs for you based on your specific needs and goals. You will have unlimited access and consultation with your trainer via email 24/7. This program has received fantastic feedback and testimonials from many users and has helped athletes all over the world achieve their goals. To learn more about this program, click the e-Training link on the home page of www.SportsWorkout.com.

Off-Season Training

The off-season is the time in any sport to build up your muscles, become more powerful, and increase muscular endurance. The off-season program consists of four 4-week routines cycled together to maximize both muscular endurance and explosive power. The first and third routines are designed to build your stamina and muscular endurance, while the second and fourth routines are designed more for power and explosion.

Variation is very important to an effective workout program. Varying your routines keeps you making progress and gains. Your body eventually will adapt to any routine it's on, so it is very important to change routines once your gains have stopped and your strength has peaked. Changing programs every four weeks is the most effective time period to follow any one routine. For more information on the importance of variation to weight training, see the section *The Declaration of Variation.*

After following the first two 4-week off-season programs, be sure to take one week away from the gym to let your muscles rest and grow stronger before beginning your final two 4-week programs.

During the off-season, you must supplement your weight-training activities with some sort of running specific activities to keep your body in proper shape.

MUSCULAR ENDURANCE TRAINING

The first and third routines of the off-season cycle are to enhance your muscular endurance. Weight training for muscular endurance differs greatly from strength and power training. Strength training builds up size, bulk, and strength; power training builds explosion, speed, and intensity; and endurance training builds your stamina by enabling your muscles to work longer without fatiguing. Weight training to increase your muscular endurance requires many slow movement repetitions to train and build your slow-twitch muscle fibers, which are responsible for increased endurance and stamina.

The keys to endurance training are as follows:

Proper breathing: Breathing properly is extremely important in endurance training. As you perform repetition after repetition, your instincts will be to hold your breath. With each and every rep, be sure to inhale while lowering the weight on the eccentric movement and exhale while raising the weights on the concentric movement. Never hold your breath.

Smooth rhythmic lifts: In endurance training, the lowering, negative part, of every rep should last at least two seconds and the raising, positive part, should be at least one second. The goal is to keep this rhythm from your first rep to your last to ensure a great workout.

Short rest times: To get the most out of endurance training, it is best if you take short rest times between sets. This gives lifting aerobic benefits because it leads to a more continuous, less sporadic workout, which keeps your heart rate up. To ensure optimal results while training for endurance, take no more than sixty seconds of rest time between sets.

Explosive-Power Training

The second and fourth routines of the cycle are designed to build speed and explosive power.

Four important aspects to explosive power training are:

Medium weights, medium reps: Training for power is quite different than training for strength. For strength training, the idea is to lift heavy weights a low number of times. Contrastingly, decreasing the weight-load and lifting between eight and fifteen repetitions is the best way to successfully train for power and explosion.

Speed and intensity: With power training, the goal is to increase the speed while lifting. Before increasing the load, you want to increase the speed at which you are performing the concentric part, or positive phase of the lift. If the load begins to feel extremely light, then follow the steps listed in the section *When to Increase* for increasing the resistance.

There are certain exercises, however, that should never be performed with speed and intensity due to the possibility of injury, or because fast movements are not as effective as slow ones. Exercises listed in our programs that should **never** be lifted with speed and intensity are:

1. Lower back exercises
2. Rotator cuff exercises
3. Mid-section exercises

Great Form: Similar to endurance training, the lowering of the weight should be smooth and slow for at least two seconds. The difference comes on the concentric part of the lift. For power training you want to raise the weights as fast and explosively as possible. This works your fast-twitch muscle fibers with the goal of increasing the speed that you can contract and move your muscles. While following power-building routines, you are required to perform the concentric part of every rep in every set with intensity and speed. On a very important note, however, you must be sure to not sacrifice form for speed.

Power exercises: Certain exercises are most beneficial and most effectively performed with speed and intensity. Olympic lifts such as push presses and power cleans, as well as body weight exercises like dips, and pull-ups are such examples because they can be performed extremely fast with enormous amounts of intensity.

You will notice that a small number of high rep exercises for endurance training are included to compliment the explosive power training. It is necessary that any explosive power weight-training program include at least some endurance building aspects in order to maintain the strength you have acquired during the endurance-training cycle. This ensures that upon completion of the first explosive power training routine, you will be able to start back up on the second endurance-building program without losing any endurance.

RUNNING OFF-SEASON PROGRAM

Weeks 1-4

Days1 & 3

muscle group	exercise	sets	reps
chest	barbell bench press	3	20
shoulders	dumbbell military press	2	20
shoulders	standing flyes	3	20
legs	leg press	3	20

Days2 & 4

muscle group	exercise	sets	reps
back	wide-grip pull ups	2	failure
bi's/forearms	hammer curls	2	20
legs	leg curls	3	20
legs	calf raises	3	20

Weeks 5-8

Days1 & 3

muscle group	exercise	sets	reps
chest	dumbbell bench press	3	15
chest	dumbbell incline bench press	2	15
shoulders	standing flyes	3	15
legs	leg press	3	15
shoulders/triceps	dips	2	failure
legs	lunges	2	15

Days2 & 4

muscle group	exercise	sets	reps
back	wide-grip pull-ups	2	failure
biceps/forearms	hammer curls	2	15
legs	leg curls	3	15
legs	calf raises	3	15
back	seated cables rows	3	15
biceps	dumbbell curls	2	15

Weeks 9-12

Days1 & 3

muscle group	exercise	sets	reps
Legs	Squats	3	20
Legs	Leg Press	3	20
Legs	Lunges	3	20
Legs	Leg Extensions	3	20
Legs	Leg Curls	3	20
Legs	Calf Raises	3	20

Days2 & 4

muscle group	exercise	sets	reps
Chest	Dumbbell Bench Press	3	20
Chest	Incline Flyes	3	20
Back	One Arm Dumbbell Rows	3	20
Back	Seated Cable Rows	3	20
Shoulders	Dumbbell Military Press	3	20
Shoulders	Upright Rows	3	20

Weeks 13-16

Days1 & 3

muscle group	exercise	sets	reps
chest	barbell bench press	3	15
chest	dumbbell incline bench press	2	15
shoulders	standing flyes	3	15
legs	leg press	3	15
shoulders/triceps	dips	2	failure
legs	lunges	2	15

Days2 & 4

muscle group	exercise	sets	reps
back	wide-grip pull-ups	2	failure
biceps/forearms	hammer curls	2	15
legs	leg curls	3	15
legs	standing calf raises	3	15
back	seated cable rows	3	15
biceps	dumbbell curls	2	15

In-Season Training

Maintenance Training

While in season, the preferred method of training is for maintenance. The goal of in-season weight training is to maintain the gains you have acquired during the off-season, while being careful not to over train and become stale. When you become stale, your abilities and performance as an athlete decrease drastically. Lifting weights more than twice a week and practicing on a daily basis is more than enough to over train many people.

In order to maintain the endurance and explosion added in the off-season, in-season maintenance training calls for working out your major muscle groups two days a week. This type of training is twice a week because it is the least number of days required to lift while still maintaining your gains. Training your muscles only once a week can cause them to lose the gains that they have acquired. The in-season routine includes maintenance exercises for endurance, strength, and explosive power elements so that nothing is lost during the season. If you wish, you can perform the in-season routine using a *circuit training* format. For more information on circuit training, see the *Training Techniques* section.

Running Preseason Program

Maintenance training

Train two days per week

Odd Weeks

Days 1 & 2

muscle group	exercise	sets	reps
chest	barbell bench press	3	20,20,20
back	one-arm dumbbell rows	3	20,20,20
shoulders	dips	3	20,20,20
legs	squats	3	20,20,20
legs	lunges	3	20,20,20
legs	standing calf raises	2	20,20

Even Weeks

Days 1 & 2

muscle group	exercise	sets	reps
chest	incline flyes	3	20,20,20
back	seated cable rows	3	20,20,20
shoulders	front raises	3	20,20,20
legs	leg press	3	20,20,20
legs	leg curls	3	20,20,20
legs	standing calf raises	2	20,20

Remember to:

Train your abs prior to each training session

Stretch your muscles directly after each training session

In the support phase, the leading foot should land on the ground slightly ahead of the athlete's center of gravity (slightly in front of the hips). The foot should be driven down towards the ground by the hip extensor muscles; the hamstrings and gluteal muscles should be performing the majority of the work during the hip extension. The quadriceps (knee extensors) are also important at foot contact since they keep the athlete's knee from flexing excessively and dissipating elastic energy. As the foot contacts the ground it should be dorsiflexed, with the big toe pulled up towards the shinbone. This helps to maximize the amount of energy that can be stored by the calf muscles and then released to generate propulsion in a later phase of the running stride. The outside of the forefoot, not the heel, should contact the ground.

The athlete should then think about pulling himself over the support foot. The athlete should continue exerting force with the hip and knee extensors until his center of gravity passes over the support foot. At this point, the runner should focus on plantarflexing the foot (pointing the toes) with the calf muscles. When the toes leave the ground, the support phase has ended.

As an athlete enters the recovery phase, the ankle should immediately be dorsiflexed with the big toe pulled up toward the shin. As the foot leaves the ground, the athlete should flex the knee and bring the heel up towards the hips/ buttocks as quickly as possible. This helps to "make the leg shorter" and allows the athlete to swing the recovery leg forward faster than he or she could if the limb was kept straight during the recovery phase. Remember, speed is what we are looking for, so even relatively "small" things like flexing the leg can help a runner gain valuable time in a race or competition. As the heel is drawn towards the hip, the leg should be swung forward. The athlete should imagine he is trying to step over the opposite knee with the ankle. This will keep the leg "short" and speed high for as long as possible. As the ankle steps over the opposite knee the athlete should begin unfolding, or extending, the swing leg. It should be noted that the hip and knee extension that occur during this phase are due to a transfer of momentum, not an active contraction of the lower limb muscles8. As the leg unfolds and the athlete prepares for the next support phase, he should focus on again activating the hip extensors to drive the foot down toward the ground.

In addition to the lower body action, there are a few other pointers that an athlete should focus on. The first of these is posture. The athlete should run with the trunk erect. The head should be level and the hips should remain tall with very little vertical movement. Second, arm swing contributes to running speed. The athlete should focus on driving the arms both backward and forward to provide balance and generate momentum. The elbow angle should range from 60 degrees in front to 140 degrees in back8 and the athlete should avoid swinging the arms across the midline of the body. Obviously an athlete has to think about a lot of things going on in a short period of time when sprinting. This can be an overwhelming skill for many athletes to learn. Drills are a valuable tool and can aid the athlete in the learning and perfecting of specific running skills. Drills can help in the development of "ideal" sprinting technique and speed9. Note that while drills are important in the development of technique, and while they serve as a useful tool in the warm up, they are not a substitute for actual running and sprint training. By definition, drills are a part of the movement. Remember that the entire skill must be put together and practiced in order for an athlete to become faster.

Sprint Technique Drills

The following technique drills will be described in this article:

Ankling,

Butt kicks, and

A drills.

Ankling Drill

"Ankling" teaches an athlete how to lift the foot off the ground during the running motion. During ankling, the knees should remain straight. The athlete should step forward with the right leg with the foot dorsiflexed and big toe lifted up towards the shin. The outside of the right forefoot should contact the ground just in front of the athlete's center of gravity. The athlete should pull himself over the foot. As the athlete's center of gravity passes over the right foot (i.e. when the foot is now behind the athlete), the foot should go into plantarflexion (pointing the toes and pushing off the ground) until it leaves the ground. As the right foot leaves the ground, the ankle should immediately be dorsiflexed and the big toe should be lifted up in preparation for moving it in front of the athlete again. Begin practicing this drill with just the right foot for 10 B 20 yards. Then perform it with the left foot. After the athlete is comfortable with this approach, have him perform this drill alternating between the right and left sides.

Butt Kick Drill

"Butt kick" drills that are performed for running are slightly different than what most of us are used to. The goal of butt kicks is to teach the athlete to lift the heel up to the hips quickly during the recovery phase of running. The athlete should step forward with his or her right leg with the foot dorsiflexed and big toe lifted up, and proceed through the support phase as was discussed in the ankling drill above. As the right foot leaves the ground, it should immediately be dorsiflexed and the big toe should be lifted up. The heel should quickly be brought up to the athlete's hip. Note that as this is done the right knee will be lifted up. Unlike more traditional butt kick drills, the goal here is not to stretch the quadriceps, it is to practice getting the heel to the hips as quickly as possible. Initially this drill should be performed with the right leg for 10 B 20 yards. The athlete should then perform it with the left leg. After the athlete is comfortable with this approach, he should perform the drill alternating between the right and left sides.

A Drills

"A drills" combine the skills learned through ankling and butt kicks and add the high knee action that is important for running. Focusing on the right leg, proceed through the foot contact and support phase as described in the ankling drill above. As the right foot leaves the ground it should immediately be dorsiflexed and the big toe should be lifted up. The heel should quickly be brought up to the athlete's hip. As the heel is brought to the hip, the leg should be swung forward attempting to lift the knee as high as possible. When the knee is in its highest position, the foot should still be dorsiflexed with the big toe lifted up. As the leg is swung forward, the leg will naturally start to "unfold." Once the limb has swung forward the athlete should drive the foot down, using the hip extensor muscles.

The athlete should practice this drill as a "walk," initially with the right side, for 10 B 20 yards. The athlete should then switch to the left side. When the athlete is comfortable with this, he should alternate between the right and left sides. When the athlete is comfortable with the A Walk, he can make it more difficult by performing the drill as a "skip." Initially the athlete should train first the right side, then the left. Once he or she is comfortable then he may alternate between the right and left sides.

SUMMARY

Being able to run fast is extremely important for success in many sports. While many factors may be trained to help improve running speed, technique is one of the most trainable and one of the most important. Solid technique will result in a faster, more efficient runner. Poor technique will limit an athlete's speed. To help an athlete master the skill, the sprinting motion may be broken down into drills that train parts of the motion. Drills simplify a complicated skill, helping with mastery. They may also serve as warm up and conditioning exercises.

References

Barbaro R. (2000). *Elements of speed development. In Jarver, J. (Ed.) Sprints and Relays 5th Edition.* Mountain View, CA: TAFNEWS Press, pg. 15 -18.

Cunningham M. (2001). *Pure speed training. Coaches Review,* 74(2):26 -B 28.

Faccioni A. (1995). *Assisted and resisted methods for speed development.* In Jarver, J. (Ed.) *Sprints and Relays 4th Edition.* Mountain View, CA: *TAFNEWS Press,* pg. 63 - 69.

Jarver J. (1978). *Sprinting in a nutshell.* In Jarver, J. (Ed.) *Sprints and Relays 1st Edition.* Mountain View, CA: *TAFNEWS Press*, pg. 9 - 13.

Kumagai K, Abe T, Brechue WF, Ryoshi T, Takano S, Mizuno M. (2000). *Sprint performance is related to muscle fascicle length in male 100-m sprinters. Journal of Applied Physiology,* 88:811 - 816.

McFarlane B. (1995). *Speed - A basic and advanced technical model. In Jarver, J. (Ed.) Sprints and Relays 4th Edition.* Mountain View, CA: *TAFNEWS Press*, pg. 14 - 19.

McFarlane B. (1987). *A look inside the biomechanics of speed.* NSCA Journal, 9(5):35 B 42.

USA Track and Field. (2001). *Coaching Education Program Level II Course: Sprints, Hurdles, Relays.*

West T, Robson S. (2000). *Running drillsCare we reaping the benefits?* In Jarver J. (Ed.) *Sprints and Relays 5th Edition*. Mountain View, CA: *TAFNEWS Press*, pg. 64 B 67.

About the Author

John M. Cissik, MS, CSCS, NSCA-CPT runs Fitness and Conditioning Enterprises, which specializes in speed and agility instruction for young athletes. He is the NSCA's State Director for Texas and is a Level II Coach (Sprints) with USA Track and Field

---

This article originally appeared in NSCA's Performance Training Journal, a publication of the National Strength and Conditioning Association.

Nutrition for Ultra-Endurance Athletes

This article was written by Brian Zehetner MS, RD, CSCS

An in-depth look at all of the nutritional considerations for competing in ultra-marathon events. Topics include hydration, pre/post event eating, and carbs.

USA Today recently came out with their top 10 most difficult things to do in sports-- # 7 was running a marathon. This seems like a pretty daunting task, but imagine swimming 2.4 miles and biking 112 miles before ever starting that run. This is exactly what an ironman triathlete has to do just to finish their event. Keep in mind, the fastest athlete will finish a race in 8 or 9 hours; a true test of strength, endurance and willpower.

Nutrition is one of the key factors in determining where you will finish, or if you will even finish at all. Let's take a look at various aspects of nutrition in relation to these ultra-endurance events.

Fluids

An athlete's hydration status is the single most important factor affecting overall performance. Numerous studies have shown that an individual's endurance gradually decreases the more they become dehydrated. Dehydration is usually a result of sweat loss, expiration, and inadequate fluid intake. If this trend progresses, serious medical complications can result. For example, a 3% decrease in total body weight has been shown to adversely affect performance, while a 5% decrease in weight can cause heat cramps and nausea (1). If proper fluid replacement isn't started, this could eventually lead to heat exhaustion, heat stroke, and possibly death. Keep in mind, the best ways to evaluate hydration status are through weight lost and the color and quantity of urine.

Luckily, most athletes that compete in ironman triathlons are aware of the dangers of dehydration. The same cannot be said for the dangers of overhydration. This is much less common, but is gaining more attention because of the popularity of ultra-endurance events. Overhydration usually occurs when an athlete is performing in hot weather, is sweating profusely, and is replacing lost fluids with plain water. When an athlete loses sweat, they are also losing large amounts of sodium, which is the main electrolyte involved in fluid balance. This sodium loss, coupled with minimal replacement from water, can lead to hyponatremia or low serum sodium levels in the body. This is a serious condition which requires immediate medical attention.

The best way to prevent complications from both dehydration and hyponatremia is to drink adequate fluids early and often, preferably those containing electrolytes such as sodium and potassium. Research has shown that athletes competing longer than 6-8 hours may need up to 1 gram of sodium per hour to replace losses (2). Some of this can be replaced by using sports drinks (i.e. Gatorade and Powerade) before and during the event. Sodium has a dual role in these beverages whereby it improves flavor and helps increase blood plasma volume (3). It's important to remember that the sodium in these drinks may not be enough for repletion needs; some athletes also eat sodium-containing foods and/or use salt tablets toward the end of an event.

Below you will find hydration guidelines for before, during, and after ironman events (4).

Before Event - 16 oz. 2 hours prior, then 4-8 oz. 5-15 minutes prior to start
During Event - 5-10 oz. every 15-20 minutes
After Event - 16-20 oz. per lb. of body weight lost

Energy

Triathletes expend an incredible amount of energy during their training and, in turn, have to consume plenty of calories on a daily basis to stay in peak form. Energy demands can be quite variable and depend upon the duration, intensity and type of exercise training (5). One ultra-endurance athlete competed in a run around Australia and ran an average of 70-90 kilometers per day (80 km equals approx. 45 miles) and consumed an average of 6,321 calories per day. It's hard to believe he needed this much energy, given the fact that his basal metabolic rate was estimated to be 1597 calories per day (6). Trying to match calories in with calories out is a difficult challenge. These athletes often need to eat several meals a day and may consume a variety of nutrient-dense foods and liquid shakes. Another factor affecting performance is the actual nutrient breakdown of the diet in terms of carbohydrates, fats and proteins.

Carbohydrates are the foundation of any nutrition regimen when training for an ironman triathlon. Unfortunately, your body only has a limited amount of carbohydrate reserve for endurance events. As an example, a 150 lb. man has approximately 1400 calories of muscle glycogen (stored sugar), 320 calories of liver glycogen and 80 calories of blood glucose (1). For comparison, this same individual would have almost an unlimited supply of fat calories to use for energy. As the intensity of exercise increases during training, more carbohydrate will be used for energy because it can be processed faster. However, when the muscle and liver stores are depleted, the body will have to pull from the blood sugar. When this happens, you are on steady path toward fatigue. This is what some of us like to call Ahitting the wall."

One way to avoid this decrease in performance is to consume adequate carbohydrates before and during training and events. Another way is to maximize muscle and liver glycogen by carbo-loading. This involves tapering training one to two weeks out from an event and then maintaining a high carbohydrate diet (usually 70% of calories). Eating a meal three to four hours before an event is also part of this loading regimen and can result in improvements in endurance (5). This is a very common practice among ironman triathletes. It's important to note that chronic fatigue can still occur if glycogen is not repleted after exercise. Consuming adequate carbohydrates after exercise sessions will help prepare you for the next training day.

Below you will find daily carbohydrate recommendations, in addition to that needed before, during and after ironman events (1).

Daily Needs - 3.0 to 5.0 gms per lb. of body weight per day
Before Event - 0.5 to 2.0 gms per lb. of body weight (1-4 hours prior)
During Event - 30-75 gms per hour
After Event -0.5 gms per lb. of body weight every 2 hours (recovery)

Until now, the focus has been on carbohydrates, however fat is one of the main reasons that triathletes are able to compete for several hours at a time. As an athlete's effort becomes more steady state, fat becomes a major contributor to energy utilization, in turn sparing carbohydrate for when the intensity picks back up. The guideline for fat intake is usually estimated to be at least 0.5 gms per lb. of body weight per day, very similar to a typical heart-healthy diet (4). This is because the body has abundant stores of fat and can utilize this for energy. The dietary fat is important because we need the essential fatty acids, which have several functions in the body.

Protein is the last of the macronutrients that a triathlete needs for optimal performance. This nutrient is not typically known as a major energy contributor during exercise, but in the fed state, it may provide up to 5% of the fuel used. As exercise duration increases, protein utilization can increase as well, maintaining blood glucose through a conversion process in the liver (7). It is important for ironman triathletes to consume protein with their meals, especially during recovery, as this will help to repair injured tissues. The typical recommendation for protein intake is 0.55 to 0.65 gms per lb. of body weight per day; more than the RDI, but less than what is recommended for strength and power athletes (4).

References

Clark, N. *Nancy Clark's Sports Nutrition Guidebook.* 2nd ed. Champaign, IL: Human Kinetics; 1997.

Clark, N., Tobin J. Jr., Ellis, C. *Feeding the Ultra-Endurance Athlete: Practical Tips and a Case Study.* Journal of the American Dietetic Association. 92: 1258-1262, 1992.

Rehrer, NJ. *The Maintenance of Fluid Balance During Exercise.* International Journal of Sports Medicine. 15: 122-125, 1994.

Rosenbloom, CA. Sports Nutrition: *A Guide for the Professional Working with Active People.* 3rd ed. Chicago, IL: The American Dietetic Association; 2000.

Applegate, EA. *Nutritional Considerations for Ultra-Endurance Performance.* International Journal of Sport Nutrition. 1: 118-126, 1991.

Hill, R. J., W. Davies, Peter S. *Energy Expenditure During 2 Weeks of an Ultra-Endurance Run Around Australia. Medicine & Science in Sports & Exercise.* 33: 148-151, 2001.

ACSM, ADA, Dietitians of Canada. *Nutrition and Athletic Performance.* Medicine & Science in Sports & Exercise. 32: 2130-2145, 2000.

Members Only Area

The articles you have just read were taken from Ryan Lee's sport-specific membership.

This member's only resource has over **10,000** pages of sports-training programs, articles, and tips written by many of the world's top authorities on sports fitness training.

"This Sport-Specific membership is simply the best and most complete sports training resource I've ever used. If you are serious about improving your sports performance ***I highly recommend joining today!***"

Duane Carlisle

NFL Philadelphia Eagles Speed Consultant

"I was just introduced to your site by a colleague of mine and I wanted to let you know how impressed I was. ***You have a wonderful site... I will certainly recommend that my athletes check out your site.***"

Matt Nichol

NHL Toronto Maple Leafs Head Strength Coach

"The site is an ***amazing collection of high-end quality information****. The valued access to the collection of data and articles here far exceeds the membership fee. Great work. Thanks again."*

Jamie Roche

Hebron Academy, Anatomy & Physiology Teacher, Coach Baseball, Soccer & Hockey

"This is by far the ***most comprehensive site any strength and speed coach could ever want****. Great job Guys!!!"*

Jude Massillon

Professional Strength Coach to Several Track/Field Olympians and over 40 NFL 1st Round Draft Choices

Take a free tour to see all of the benefits members get by visiting **www.SportsWorkout.com** and clicking the 'Members Only' link.

Get **$5** off and an **extra 6 months free** with Promo Code **MEM439**

Go to **www.SportsWorkout.com** or call **1-866-SWORKOUT (796-7568)** to Order!

Part II

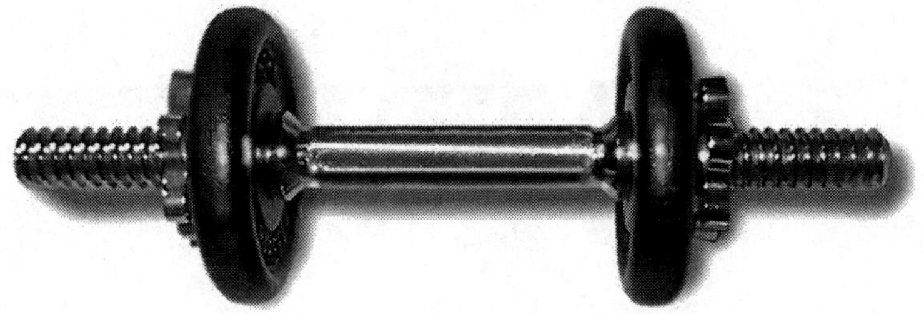

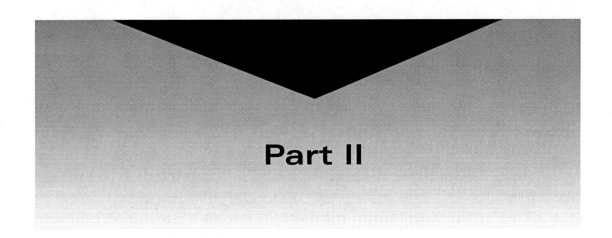

Getting Started

WARMING UP

Warming up is an essential part of a weight-training routine. *A warm-up activity can be any type of low-level activity as long as it loosens up your body, gets your blood flowing, and prepares your body for the workout.* Warming up is absolutely necessary if you plan to lift heavy weights. To walk into the gym and attempt *to max* out (lift the maximum amount of weight you can handle) without first warming up can cause injury because your body is not ready for the physical stress of a weight-training routine. In general, there are two major types of warming up, which are listed below.

A **full body warm-up** is anything that increases your blood flow and literally warms you up. Examples of full-body warm-up activities include low-intensity activities such as jogging or riding the bike for five to ten minutes prior to lifting weights. Other examples include about five to ten minutes of an abdominal routine, swimming a few laps, or even some full-body stretching.

An **exercise-specific warm-up** is properly executed by performing a light-weight set (group of repetitions) of an exercise before going into your prescribed routine for that same exercise with heavier weights. Ten repetitions are usually enough for a warm-up set. Basing your exercise-specific warm-up set on half of your *one-rep max* is the best technique. Your one-rep max is the maximum weight you can lift one time. Performing an exercise-specific warm-up increases your blood flow to the *active muscles*, that is, the muscles you are using.

Benefits of Warming Up One major benefit of warming up is that it helps reduce the likelihood of pulls, tears, and other injuries, which can be painful and hamper your future training. Another major benefit of warming up is that it loosens your muscles and allows you to lift heavier weights. Heavier weights, in turn, put more resistance on your muscles, which forces you work to harder and gives you a better workout.

Cooling Down

Cooling-down activities come directly after your weight-training session. While cooling down, the goal is, again, to loosen up your muscles. In this book, cool-down activities are synonymous with stretching exercises. Cooling-down activities are important because they can prevent soreness in the days following a weight-training session. They also increase your range of motion, helping you become more flexible, which can prevent injuries both in the weight room and in athletics. Because flexibility and range of motion are so important for all sports, stretching is a vital part of a complete workout program and should never be ignored.

There are numerous benefits to stretching and it is most effective during or after your workout. Stretching increases your range of motion and ***stretching can be effective in injury reduction.*** Proper stretching *may* also be effective in reducing soreness from weight training by helping to remove the anaerobic waste product—lactate—from your muscles.

Range of motion is essential for all sports and physical activities, and stretching is the way to increase it. It is a myth that weight training automatically makes you stiff and decreases your flexibility. Training ***antagonistic,*** or opposite, muscle groups in the same session actually stretches your muscles and helps increase your range of motion. An example of an antagonistic muscle group is the biceps and triceps. As the biceps contract, the triceps extend, which gives them a nice, full stretch.

Abs

Having a tight stomach, strong lower back, and incredible six-pack is important for both personal and athletic reasons. The exercises provided in this book will have you training properly and building picture-perfect abs. Lower back and oblique exercises are also incorporated with the abs routine so that your entire torso becomes stronger. Having strong abdominals is essential for high sports performance. With tight abs and a strong lower back, you will be able to run faster and become more explosive. You will also be able to make quicker movements with your torso, which leads to jumping higher and making sharper turns and cuts. Your midsection connects your upper body to your lower body, and it allows you to apply the strength and power collectively in both areas. A stronger midsection will increase your athletic capabilities.

By nature, the muscles in your midsection are different from the other muscles in your body and need to be trained differently in order to achieve maximum results. To train your abs properly, you need the following:

1. Slow movements: Abs are made up mostly of slow-twitch muscle fibers, which requires them to be trained with slow movements for optimal results.

2. Quantity and consistency: Abdominals need to be trained for muscular endurance, not muscular strength, which requires many, many repetitions that can be performed daily.

3. Variety: Your midsection consists of different areas, each of which requires different exercises. To train each area, you need to perform a variety of exercises. Variety with any exercise is an essential part of muscle building and athletic training. Variety allows you to build and tone every part of the muscle you are training.

To keep things simple, this book refers to the areas of the abdomen as the:

- **Upper Abs**
- **Lower Abs**
- **Obliques**

Preferred Order of Training

Lower abs and oblique exercises are *compound exercises,* that is, they train more than one muscle group at a time. These exercises also train your upper abs. Upper abs exercises, on the other hand, strictly isolate your upper abs. In order to avoid fatigue in the upper abs, which are being worked in every type of abdominal exercise, and could prevent proper lower abs and obliques training, you should train the lower abs first, then the obliques, and lastly the upper abs.

The preferred order of training your abdominals is as follows:

- **Lower Abs**
- **Obliques**
- **Upper Abs**

Note: You can train your lower back before or after performing your abdominal exercises, depending on your personal preference.

Training your midsection for at least five minutes prior to lifting is a great way to warm up because you are both warming yourself up by increasing your blood flow, and you are also building and toning your entire midsection. This can be thought of this as killing two birds with one stone. Perform each exercise slowly and smoothly for one full minute without rest. Rest for 30 seconds between exercises.

Listed below are descriptions and pictures demonstrating exactly how to perform each of the recommended midsection exercises. Do not be overwhelmed by the vast number of recommended exercises. You only need to pick four or five of them for each warm-up routine. As your midsection becomes stronger, you should increase the number of exercises you perform so that you continue progressing in strength. Vary your routine constantly by choosing four or five exercises to warm up with one day and a completely new set of four or five exercises the next day.

ABS EXERCISES

Definition: *Prime movers* are the muscles being directly trained in the exercise.

Standard Sit-ups

Prime Movers: Upper abs

Starting Position: Lie flat on your back with your knees bent and the soles of your feet flat on the floor. Elevate your tailbone about one inch above the floor. Place your hands on your ears.

Use your abs to lift the upper half of your body as high as you can, hold the position for a second or two, then slowly return to your starting position.

Tip: By keeping your tailbone elevated, you are working your lower abs, which is a target area for many people.

Standard Crunches

Prime Movers: Upper abs

Starting Position: Lie flat on your back with your feet and knees elevated so that your shins are parallel with the floor. Elevate your tail-bone about one inch above the floor. Place your hands on your ears.

Use your abs to lift the upper half of your body. Once you've lifted your shoulders about thirty degrees off the floor, hold the position for a second or two, then slowly return to the starting position and repeat.

Oblique Crunches

Prime Movers: Obliques

Starting Position: Lie on your left side with your legs slightly bent, knees elevated about an inch or two above the floor, and your hands on your ears. Twist your torso to the right and do your best to keep your upper back and shoulders parallel with the floor.

Use your obliques and upper abs to lift your upper body as high as you can and hold for a second or two. Return slowly to the starting position, and repeat. Then perform this exercise lying on your right side.

Tailbone Lifts

Prime Movers: Lower abs

Starting Position: Lie flat on your back with your feet and knees elevated so that your shins are parallel with the floor and place your hands on your ears.

With your stomach flexed, use your lower abs to raise your tailbone an inch or two off the floor. Hold that position for a second or two before lowering your tailbone back to the floor. Be sure to keep your upper body in the same position throughout the entire range of motion.

Elbow to Knee Sit-ups

Prime Movers: Entire torso

Starting Position: Lie flat on your back with your knees bent and the soles of your feet flat the floor. Place your hands on your ears.

Use your abs to raise your upper body forward while lifting your left foot off the floor so that your knee comes towards your head. Touch your knee to its opposite elbow. Hold that position for a second or two with your abs flexed. Slowly lower yourself back to the starting position and repeat the same movements with your right knee and left elbow.

Bicycles

Prime Movers: Entire torso

Starting Position: Lie flat on your back with your knees bent, legs extended, feet elevated a few inches above the floor, and your hands on your ears.

Use your abs to raise your upper body forward. At the same time, begin to slowly pump your legs one by one as if you were riding a bicycle. As your knee comes towards to your head, touch your raised knee to its opposite elbow. Hold that position for a second or two with your abs flexed. Go back to the starting point and repeat the same movements with your other knee and elbow.

Side Bends

Prime Movers: Obliques

Starting Position: Standing upright, hold a dumbbell in your left hand and place your right hand on your head.

Lean your upper body a few inches to the left and use your obliques on the right side of your body to return to the starting position.

Good Mornings

Prime Movers: Lower back

Starting Position: Stand upright with your feet close together. Rest a barbell behind your neck on your traps. Keep your head tilted back and your back completely straight.

Slowly bend at the waist until you form a ninety-degree angle with your lower body. Slowly return to the starting position and repeat.

Hyperextensions

Prime Movers: Lower back

Starting Position: Lie face down on a hyperextension bench. Bend at the waist with your upper body hanging straight down and your hands placed behind your neck. Tilt your head back and keep your back straight.

Slowly raise your upper body until it is parallel with the floor and level with your lower body. Slowly return to the starting position and repeat.

Tip for hyperextensions and the preceding exercise, good mornings: Do not arch your back at any point because it can result in a painful injury

Reach Throughs

Prime Movers: Upper and lower abs

Starting Position: Lie flat on your back with your legs extended, slightly spread apart, and elevated a few inches above the floor. Extend both your arms behind your head.

Use your abs to lift the upper half of your body up and bring your knees upward so that your shins are parallel with the floor. Simultaneously extend your arms directly in front of you, between your legs. Hold the position for a second or two, slowly return to the starting position, and repeat.

Leg Raises

Prime Movers: Lower abs

Starting Position: Lie on the floor with your legs extended and your shoulders and head tilted forward off the floor, putting stress on your upper abs. Place your hands underneath your tailbone to keep it slightly elevated above the floor. Keep your upper body stationary, hands underneath your tailbone, and legs locked throughout the entire range of motion.

Raise your legs off the floor until they form a ninety-degree angle with the floor, allowing your tailbone and lower back to come off the floor in the process. Slowly lower your legs back to the starting position and repeat.

Tip: To get your legs that high may require a thrust from your abs, which in this case is okay.

Intercostal Pull Overs

Prime Movers: Intercostals

Starting Position: Lie on a bench with a barbell resting on your chest and your head slightly off the bench. Hold the bar with an overhand grip.

Slowly lift and lower the bar just over and behind your head until you feel a nice stretch in your chest. At this point raise the bar back over your head to the starting position.

Tip: If having your head partially off of the bench feels awkward and difficult, then perform this exercise with your head resting on the bench.

Stretching

Stretching is an absolutely crucial part to weight training for sports. It loosens you up, increases your range of motion, and may reduce the chance of injury and soreness in the days following a workout or athletic competition. Stretching is directly related to flexibility. This section goes into depth on how to properly stretch your muscles during or after a workout.

Everyone knows that stretching increases flexibility, but not everyone knows that lack of stretching decreases flexibility.

The recommended time for holding each stretch is ten seconds, resting thirty seconds between stretches. While holding a stretch, do not bounce; the stretch is less effective and can cause painful injuries. For every exercise, stretch as far as you can until you feel slight discomfort in the targeted areas. Go no farther once you reach that point. Hold that position for ten seconds as steadily as you can. Proper breathing and technique are extremely important. Do not hold your breath at any time during the stretch. The recommended stretching exercises and their descriptions and pictures are listed on the following pages.

Hamstrings, Legs Crossed

Muscles stretched: Hamstrings.

Starting position: Stand upright and cross your left foot over your right, keeping your legs straight. Bending at the waist, reach as far down as you can, and hold. Repeat with other leg.

Hamstrings, Legs Spread

Muscles stretched: Hamstrings, groin

Starting Position: Stand upright and spread your legs slightly wider than shoulder width, keeping them straight.

Bending at the waist, reach as far down as you can to the outside leg and hold. Repeat to the other leg, then reach straight down. Rest between each stretch.

Hurdler Stretch

Muscles stretched: Hamstrings, quadriceps.

Starting Position: Sit on the floor with your right leg extended in front of you and your left leg bent at the knee and pointing behind you.

Bend at the waist and reach as far forward as you can to your right leg and hold.

Repeat with left leg extended.

Sit and Reach

Muscles stretched: Hamstrings, lower back.

Starting Position: Sit on the floor with both legs extended in front of you.

Reach forward as far as you can towards your feet, and hold.

Standing Quad Stretch

Muscles stretched: Quadriceps.

Starting Position: Stand upright on your left leg.

Grab your right ankle and pull it back as far as you can towards your buttocks and hold.

Repeat with other leg.

Neck Rolls

Muscles stretched: Neck.

Starting Position: Stand upright with your hands on your hips.

Slowly roll your head clockwise in a circular motion using your full range of motion for ten rotations. Repeat going counterclockwise.

Across Body Arm Pulls

Muscles stretched: Shoulders, upper back

Starting Position: Stand or sit upright with your back straight. Reach across your body with your left arm. Use your right hand to lightly pull and stretch the left arm as far and as close to your body as you can and hold. Repeat with other arm.

Overhead Arm Pulls

Muscles stretched: Triceps, shoulders, upper back.

Starting Position: Stand or sit upright with your back straight.

Reach up and behind your neck with your left arm. Use your right hand to lightly pull and stretch your left arm as far as you can and hold.

Repeat with other arm.

Butterflies

Muscles stretched: Groin, hips.

Starting Position: Sit upright with your back straight and legs tucked in. Touch the soles of your shoes together and hold your toes with your hands. Pull your feet in as close as you can to your body.

With your elbows, lightly push your knees towards the floor as far as you can and hold.

Seated Back Twists

Muscles stretched: Lower back, trunk, thighs, and hips.

Starting Position: Sit upright with your back straight and left leg extended. Bend and cross your right leg over your left. Place your left forearm on the outside of your right leg, your right hand resting palm down on the floor next to you for balance. Twist your body to the right as far as you can and hold. Repeat to the other side.

Lying Knee Grabs

Muscles stretched: Glutes, hips.

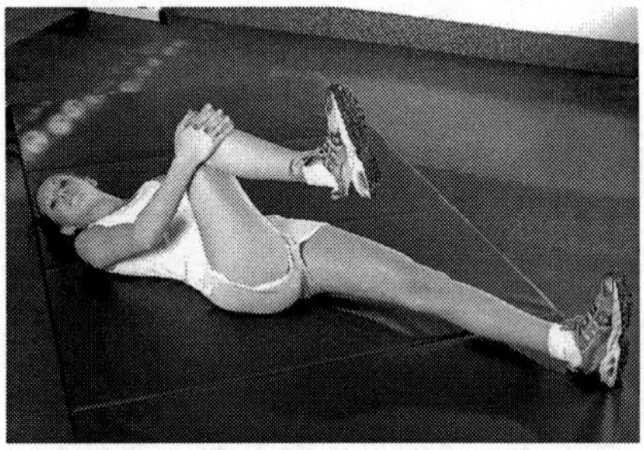

Starting Position: Lying flat on your back with your left knee bent and right leg extended, clasp your hands over the upper shin of your left knee.

Gently pull your left leg towards your chest until you feel the stretch and hold.

Repeat with other leg.

Standing Calves Stretch

Muscles stretched: Calves.

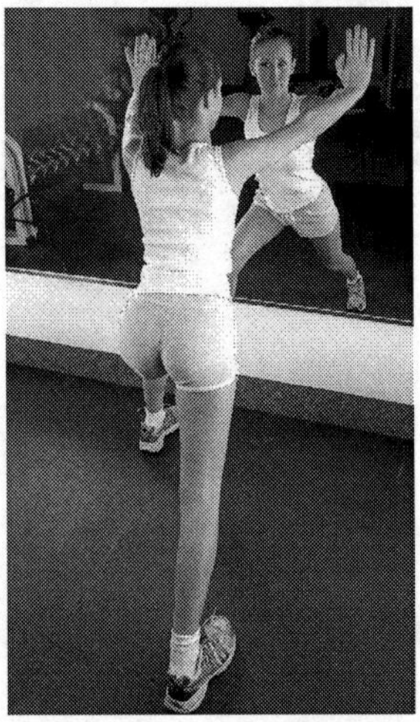

Starting Position: Stand leaning forward with your arms in front of you and your hands pushing against a wall. Place your left leg in front of the right.

Bend your left knee while keeping your right heel flat on the floor. Lean as far forward as you can while still keeping your back heel on the floor and hold.

Repeat with other leg.

Tip: This exercise also can be performed with both feet back.

Proper Form

Short- vs. Long-Term Results

In order to make the greatest gains in the least amount of time, you must perform each exercise properly. Lifting weights with bad form is very dangerous and can result in injury. Also, performing an exercise improperly is a waste of time in the gym. Though you may be able to lift heavier weights with improper form, your long-term results would suffer because you would not get as good a workout. You are better off working out for thirty minutes per day with excellent form and technique than lifting for three hours per day with improper form.

There are two movements to lifting a weight: the eccentric (negative) phase and the concentric (positive) phase.

The eccentric (negative) phase of the lift is the slow lowering of the weight. During this phase, your muscle is getting longer while still contracting. For example, in the bench press the eccentric phase occurs when you slowly lower the bar to your chest, lengthening your pectorals and triceps. Regardless of your purpose, the eccentric phase of the lift should always be slow and smooth, lasting at least two seconds. Always inhale while performing the eccentric phase of the lift.

For the best results, the eccentric phase of every lift should last for at least two seconds.

The concentric (positive) phase of the lift is the exertion phase, or actual lifting of the weight. During this phase, the muscle shortens and the muscle cells contract. For example, in the bench press the concentric phase occurs when you lift the bar up from your chest so that your pectorals and triceps contract. The concentric phase of every lift should last at least one second unless you are training for power and explosion, where you lift the weight concentrically as fast as you can. Always exhale while performing the concentric phase of the lift.

Proper Breathing

DO NOT HOLD YOUR BREATH while lifting! Holding your breath can build up pressure in your body. Although extremely rare, if the pressure becomes extraordinarily intense, it can cut off blood circulation to your heart and brain. To avoid problems, just remember to breathe. Remember, you will get the most out of your lifting by inhaling on the eccentric part of the lift and exhaling while performing the concentric part of the lift.

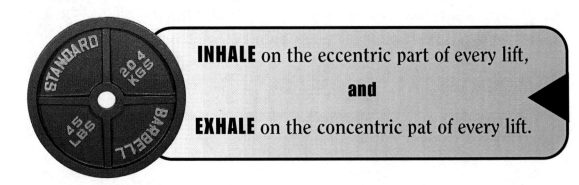

INHALE on the eccentric part of every lift,

and

EXHALE on the concentric pat of every lift.

Important note: If you have the determination to get to the gym for a set amount of time, then train with proper form and intensity so that you spend your time efficiently. Many people come home from the gym and feel a false sense of achievement simply because they had "made it to the gym." Once there, you need to work hard so you can *honestly* feel good about yourself for having taken one step closer to achieving your goals. Rather than going back to the gym over and over again to try and make up for lost time, do it right the first time.

Part III

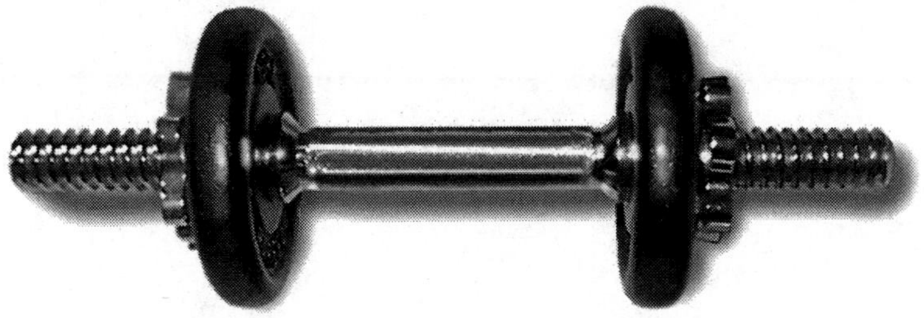

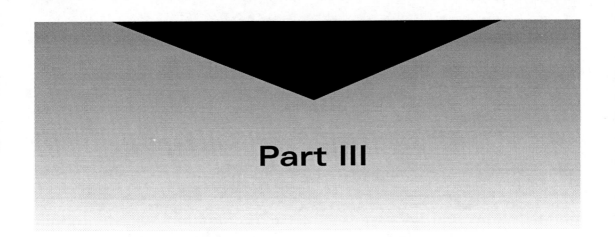

Recommended Exercises

This section provides you with every recommended weight-training exercise. You are given complete descriptions and pictures to ensure that you perform the exercises properly, safely, and effectively.

The numbers next to the exercises refer to their order of interchangeability, which is discussed in the following subsection. The muscles listed first after "prime movers" are the muscles that are being directly trained. Along with the descriptions are many helpful tips.

Substituting Similar Exercises

Our weight-training specialists did the hard work for you by strategically designing each program; all you have to do is follow them. Sometimes, however, there may be a required exercise or two that you either cannot perform physically or for which you do not have the equipment to perform. Many people struggle to do certain body weight exercises such as pull-ups or dips. Others may not have access to certain weight-training equipment such as cable or leg press machines. For these reasons, the exercises are listed for you are in order of interchangeability. If there is an exercise in your routine that you are not able to perform, substitute an exercise with a corresponding number from the same section. This substitution will ensure that you are training the same muscle groups in a similarly effective manner.

Chest Exercises

Interchangeable Chest Exercises

1 Barbell Bench Press

1 Dumbbell Bench Press

1 Pushups

2 Incline Barbell Bench Press

2 Incline Dumbbell Bench Press

3 Flyes

3 Incline Flyes

3 Cable Crossovers

Dips (can be interchanged with any chest, shoulder, or triceps exercise)

SAFETY TIP!

When using a cable machine do not lower the weights so low or fast that they hit the weight stack. This stops the fluid motion of the lift and can cause injuries.

Barbell Bench Press

Prime movers: Chest, triceps, shoulders.

Starting Position: Lie on a flat bench with your feet flat on the floor. Keep your eyes directly below the bar and your hands shoulder width apart. Lift the bar off its supports until your arms are extended.

Lift:

a. Slowly lower the bar until it grazes you chest. The bar should come to a brief, complete stop.

b. Push the bar back to full extension with the bar directly in line with your chin.

Tip: Do not arch your back to try and lift more weight because it can cause serious back problems.

Tip: A closer grip trains your inner chest and triceps well; a wider grip works your outer chest.

Dumbbell Bench Press

Prime movers: Chest, triceps, shoulders.

Starting Position: Lie on a flat bench with your feet flat on the floor. Hold the dumbbells with your arms extended.

Lift:

a. Slowly lower the dumbbells until you feel a comfortable stretch in your chest. The dumbbells should come to a brief, complete stop slightly below your chest.

b. Push the dumbbells back to full extension.

Tip: Dumbbells allow you to bring the weight lower than barbells, training your chest over the entire range of motion in ways a barbell cannot.

Pushups

Prime movers: Chest, shoulders, triceps.

Starting Position: Lie face down on the floor with your back straight and palms on the floor, shoulder width apart, your legs locked, and your toes on the floor with your heels in the air.

Lift:

a. Push your body upward off of the floor until your arms are fully extended.

b. Slowly lower yourself until your chest is about an inch from the floor with your legs remaining locked. Come to a brief, complete stop before continuing.

Tip: To really train your triceps well, put your hands together and form a triangle with your index fingers and thumbs.

Incline Barbell Bench Press

Prime movers: Upper chest, triceps, shoulders.

Starting Position: Lie on an inclined bench with your feet flat on the floor. Keep your eyes directly below the bar and your hands shoulder width apart.

Lift: Lift the bar off of its supports until your arms are extended.

a. Slowly lower the bar until it grazes your chest. The bar should come to a brief, complete stop.

b. Push the bar back to full extension with the bar directly in line with your chin.

Tip: You will not be able to lift as much as with a regular bench press. The steeper the degree of an incline, the less weight one typically is able to lift.

Incline Dumbbell Bench Press

Prime movers: Upper chest, triceps, shoulders.

Starting Position: Lie on an inclined bench with your feet flat on the floor. Hold the dumbbells with your arms extended in the starting position.

Lift:

a. Slowly lower the dumbbells until you feel a comfortable stretch in your chest. The dumbbells should come to a brief, complete stop slightly below your chest.

b. Push the dumbbells back to full extension.

Flyes

Prime movers: Chest.

Starting Position: Lie on a bench with your feet flat on the floor. Hold the dumbbells with your arms extended and your palms facing each other so that the dumbbells are touching.

Lift:

a. Slowly lower the dumbbells away from each other with your arms slightly bent. Extend the dumbbells as wide as you can until you feel a comfortable stretch in your chest.

b. The dumbbells should come to a brief, complete stop slightly below your chest with your palms facing upward. Use your chest muscles to bring the dumbbells back to the starting position the same way they were brought down.

Tip: As you bring the dumbbells together, rotating your wrists and touching the tops and bottoms of the dumbbells together is a nice change of pace and trains your muscles from different angles.

Incline Flyes

Prime movers: Chest.

Starting Position: Lie on an inclined bench with your feet flat on the floor. Hold the dumbbells with your arms extended and your palms facing each other so that the dumbbells are touching.

Lift:

a. Slowly lower the dumbbells away from each other with your arms slightly bent. Extend the dumbbells as wide as you can until you feel a comfortable stretch in your chest.

b. The dumbbells should come to a brief, complete stop slightly below your chest with your palms facing upward. Use your chest muscles to bring the dumbbells back to the starting position the same way they were brought down.

Cable Crossovers

Prime movers: Chest.

Starting Position: Stand bent slightly forward with your back straight and, with cables on both sides and slightly behind you, grab hold of the cables.

Lift:

a. With your arms slightly bent, use your chest to slowly bring the cables towards each other where they will pass each other in front of you. Cross the cables as far as you can.

b. The cables should come to a brief, complete stop. Then, slowly allow the cables to go back to the starting position the same way they were brought across.

Tip: Alternate which arm is on top and bottom for every rep to ensure both sides are getting equal training.

Dips

Prime movers: Chest, shoulders, triceps.

Starting Position: With arms extended, grip the parallel bars with both hands so that your body is elevated off the floor.

Lift:

a. With your elbows tucked in as closely as possible and your back straight, slowly lower yourself until your chin is parallel with the bars.

b. Use your chest muscles, shoulders, and triceps to push back up to full extension with your arms locked.

Tip: The farther you lean your body forward, the more your chest gets trained. As you straighten your body, your triceps begin to do the bulk of the work.

BACK (LATS) EXERCISES

Interchangeable Back (Lats) Exercises

1 Lat Pull Downs

1 Behind-the-Neck Pull Downs

1 Seated Cable Rows

1 Pull-ups

2 Bent-Over Barbell Rows

2 Bent-Over Dumbbell Rows

2 T-bar Rows

2 One-Arm Dumbbell Rows

Lat Pull Downs

Prime movers: Lats, biceps, shoulders.

Starting Position: Sit at a lat pull down machine. Keep your back straight and lean backward a few inches with your feet resting on the floor. Grab the bar with both hands, using an overhand grip.

Lift:

a. Keeping your body stationary and bending at the elbows, pull the bar down in front of your neck, squeezing your shoulder blades together until the bar grazes your chest.

b. Let the bar come to a brief, complete stop before slowly and controllably guiding it back up to its original starting position, the same way you pulled it down.

Tip: This exercise can also be performed with an underhand grip.

Tip for all pull downs and pull-ups: The wider the grip, the more you train the upper part of your back. The closer the grip, the more you train the lower part of the back.

Behind-the-Neck Pull Downs:

Prime movers: Lats, shoulders, biceps.

Starting Position: Sit upright at a lat pull down machine. Keep your back straight with your feet resting on the floor. Grab the bar with both hands, using an overhand grip.

Lift:

a. Keeping your body stationary and bending at the elbows, pull the bar down behind your neck, squeeze your shoulder blades together, and bring the bar as low as you can.

b. Let the bar come to a brief, complete stop before slowly and controllably guiding it back up to its original starting position, the same way you pulled it down.

Tip: More flexible people will be able to pull the bar down lower. Do not pull the bar down so low that it starts to feel uncomfortable. If you feel any unusually pain, DO NOT perform this exercise.

Seated Cable Rows

Prime movers: Lats, biceps, shoulders.

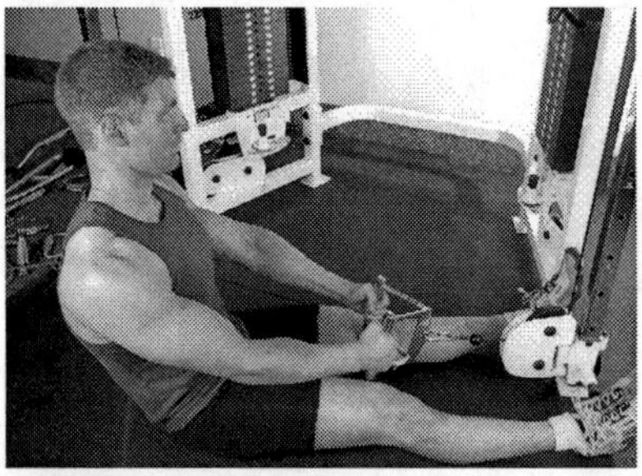

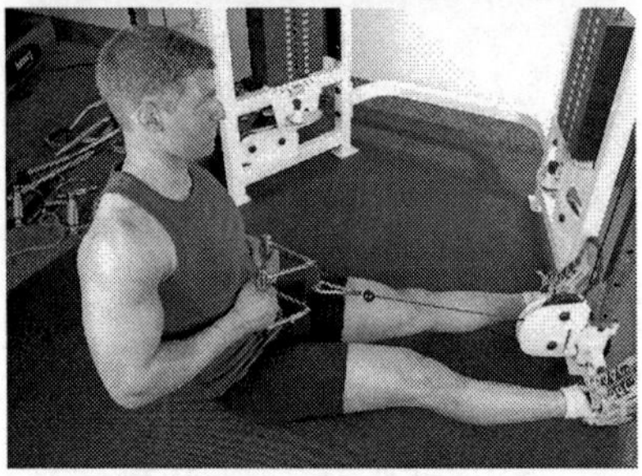

Starting Position: Sit at a row machine with your back straight, feet resting on the foot rests and legs slightly bent. Lean forward and grab the handles.

Lift:

a. Keeping your back straight, lean backward and pull the handles towards your stomach as far back as you can, squeezing your shoulder blades together.

b. Let the handles come to a brief, complete stop before slowly and controllably guiding them back up to their original starting position, the same way you pulled them up.

Pull-ups

Prime movers: Lats, biceps, shoulders

Starting Position: Grab hold of a pull-up bar using an overhand grip with your arms completely extended and feet crossed and off the floor.

Lift:

a. Keeping your body stationary, feet crossed, and bending at the elbows, pull your body up in front of the bar as high as you can, squeezing your shoulder blades together.

b. Let your body come to a brief, complete stop before slowly and controllably lowering it back up to its original starting position, the same way you pulled it up.

Tip: This exercise can also be performed behind the neck or with an underhand grip.

Tip: To train for optimal results, be sure to lower yourself all the way until your arms are nearly extended.

Bent-Over Barbell Rows

Prime movers: Lats, biceps, shoulders.

Starting Position: Standing with your knees slightly bent, feet a couple of inches apart, and bending at the waist to form an approximate ninety-degree angle, hold a bar with your arms hanging in front of you. Keep your back straight and your head tilted back.

Lift:

a. Keeping your body stationary and bending at the elbows, pull the bar up towards your stomach squeezing your shoulder blades together.

b. Let the bar come to a brief, complete stop before slowly and controllably guiding it back up to its original starting position, the same way you pulled it up.

Tip for all bent-over back exercises: Do not pull the weights towards your chest; this does not isolate your lats as well as raising the bar to your stomach.

Bent-Over Dumbbell Rows

Prime movers: Lats, biceps, shoulders.

Starting Position: Standing with your knees slightly bent, feet a couple of inches apart, and bending at the waist to form an approximate ninety-degree angle, hang your arms to the sides and hold two dumbbells with your palms facing each other. Keep your back straight and your head tilted back.

Lift:

a. Keeping your body stationary and bending at the elbows, pull the dumbbells up the sides of your body as high as you can, squeezing your shoulder blades together.

b. Let the dumbbells come to a brief, complete stop before slowly and controllably guiding them back up to their original starting position, the same way you pulled them up.

T-bar Rows

Prime movers: Lats, biceps, shoulders.

Starting Position: Standing with your knees slightly bent, feet a couple of inches apart, and bending at the waist to form a forty-five-degree angle with your floor, use an overhand grip to hold the handles of a T-bar machine, keeping the weights off of the floor. Keep your back straight and your head tilted back.

Lift:

a. Keeping your body stationary and bending at the elbows, pull the bar up towards your chest squeezing your shoulder blades together.

b. Let the bar come to a brief, complete stop before slowly and controllably guiding it back up to its original starting position, the same way you pulled it up.

Tip: If no T-bar machines are available, you can make your own using a barbell and a cable bar, as shown in the picture.

One-Arm Dumbbell Rows

Prime movers: Lats, biceps, shoulders

Starting Position: Standing with your left hand and left knee resting on a bench, bend at the waist to form an approximate ninety-degree angle. Hang your right arm to the side and hold the dumbbell with your palm facing towards your body. Keep your back straight and your head tilted back.

Lift:

a. Keeping your body stationary and bending at the elbow, pull the dumbbell up the side of your body as high as you can.

b. Let the dumbbell come to a brief, complete stop before slowly and controllably guiding it back up to its original starting position, the same way you pulled it up.

Shoulders Exercises

Interchangeable Shoulder Exercises

1 Barbell Military (Shoulder) Press

1 Dumbbell Military (Shoulder) Press

1 Push Press (Jerks)

2 Front Raises

2 Lateral Raises

2 Bent-Over Lateral Raises

2 Cable Lateral Raises

3 Standing Flyes

3 Upright Rows

4 Barbell Shrugs

4 Dumbbell Shrugs

5 Rotator Cuff Prone Position

5 Rotator Cuff On Side

Barbell Military (Shoulder) Press

Prime movers: Shoulders, triceps.

Starting Position: Stand or sit upright and hold a bar at your shoulders, using an overhand grip. Grip the bar with your hands slightly wider than shoulder width.

Lift:

a. Keeping your body still, push the bar straight up until your arms are extended.

b. Slowly lower the bar down to the original starting position.

Dumbbell Military (Shoulder) Press

Prime movers: Shoulders, triceps.

Starting Position: Stand or sit upright and hold dumbbells at your shoulders. Hold them with your hands slightly wider than shoulder width.

Lift:

a. Keeping your body still, push the dumbbells straight up until your arms are extended.

b. Slowly lower the dumbbells down to their original starting position.

Push Press (Jerks)

Prime movers: Shoulders, triceps, legs.

Starting Position: Stand with your back straight and knees slightly bent. Hold the bar at your shoulders using an overhand grip. Grip the bar with your hands slightly wider than shoulder width.

a. Explode upwards with your legs to give the bar some upward momentum. With this momentum, push the bar straight up until your arms are extended.

b. Slowly lower the bar down and return to the starting position.

Front Raises

Prime movers: Shoulders, traps.

Starting Position: Stand or sit upright and hold two dumbbells in front of you with your palms facing towards your body.

Lift:

a. With your arms remaining straight, raise the dumbbells out in front of you in one smooth, fluid motion until your hands are slightly above your shoulders.

b. Let the dumbbells come to a brief, complete stop before slowly lowering them back down to their original starting position, the same way you raised them up.

Tip for All Shoulder Raises

Once you raise your arms beyond a ninety-degree angle with your body, you begin to focus more on your traps.

Lateral Raises

Prime movers: Shoulders, traps

Starting Position: Stand or sit upright and hold two dumbbells at your sides with your palms facing your body.

Lift:

a. With your arms remaining straight, raise the dumbbells out to your sides in one smooth, fluid motion until your hands are slightly above your shoulders and slightly in front of you. As they reach this position, rotate your thumbs downward as if you are pouring a glass of water.

b. Let the dumbbells come to a brief, complete stop before slowly lowering them back down to their original starting position, the same way you raised them up.

Tip: This exercise can also be performed with your palms pointing upward towards the ceiling.

Tip for all shoulder raises: You can raise the dumbbells with both arms at the same time or alternate arms.

Bent-Over Lateral Raises

Prime movers: Shoulders, traps.

Starting Position: Stand or sit bent at the waist, keeping your back completely straight and forming a ninety-degree angle with your legs. Let your arms hang straight down in front of you with your palms facing each other.

Lift:

a. With your arms remaining straight, raise your arms out to your sides until they are parallel with your shoulders and slightly in front of you. As they reach shoulder level, rotate your thumbs downward in one smooth, fluid motion as if you are pouring a glass of water.

b. Let the dumbbells come to a brief, complete stop before slowly lowering them back down to their original starting position the same way you raised them up.

Cable Lateral Raises

Prime movers: Shoulders, traps.

Starting Position: Stand with your right arm next to a cable machine with your back straight. Grab hold of the cable with your left arm, so that your arm is hanging, slightly bent, across the front of your body. Rest the hand you are not using on your hip.

Lift:

a. Keeping your body still and your arm slightly bent, raise the cable across your body and out to the side in one motion until your hand is elevated slightly above your shoulder. As it reaches this level, rotate your thumbs downward in one smooth, fluid motion as if you are pouring a glass of water.

b. Let the cable come to a brief, complete stop before slowly lowering it back down to its original starting position the same way you raised it up.

Standing Flyes

Prime movers: Shoulders, traps.

Starting Position: Stand upright or with your knees slightly bent and bend at the waist with your back straight to form a forty-five-degree angle with your lower body. With your palms facing each other, hold two dumbbells a few inches in front of your chest with your elbows bent at ninety-degree angles.

Lift:

a. Keeping your body still and your arms bent at 90-degree angles, pull the weights upward and backward as far back as you can, squeezing your shoulder blades together.

b. Come to a brief, complete stop before slowly returning the weights back to their starting position the same way you raised them up.

Tip for standing flyes and upright rows: Avoid using your back and body momentum to complete these lifts because doing so is not an effective way of training and could cause injury.

Upright Rows

Prime movers: Shoulders, traps, biceps.

Starting Position: Stand upright with your arms hanging in front of you. Hold a barbell with an overhand grip. Your hands should be roughly eight inches apart.

Lift:

a. Keeping your body still and back straight, raise the bar upwards to your chin, keeping the bar as close to your body as you can without touching it.

b. Let the bar come to a brief, complete stop before slowly lowering it back down to its original starting position the same way you raised it up.

Barbell Shrugs

Prime movers: Traps

Starting Position: Stand upright with your arms hanging in front of you. Hold a barbell with an overhand grip, hands roughly shoulder-width apart.

Lift:

a. Keeping your body still, back straight, and arms hanging in front of you, raise only your shoulders straight up.

b. Hold the position for at least three seconds before slowly lowering your shoulders back down to the original starting position.

TIP FOR BARBELL AND DUMBBELL SHRUGS:
Keeping your head down increases your range of motion for these exercises, giving your traps a better workout.

Dumbbell Shrugs

Prime movers: Traps

Starting Position: Stand upright with arms hanging at your sides. Hold dumbbells with your palms facing each other.

Lift:

a. Keeping your body still, back straight, and arms hanging at your sides, raise only your shoulders straight up.

b. Hold the position for at least three seconds before slowly lowering your shoulders back down to the original starting position.

Rotator Cuff Prone Position

Area trained: Rotator cuff.

Starting Position: Lie face down on a bench with one arm extended to the side so that your upper arm is parallel to the floor. Bend your arm at a ninety-degree angle so that your hand is hanging with your palm facing behind you. Hold a light weight in that hand.

Lift:

a. Keeping everything else stationary, rotate your forearm upward until it becomes parallel with the ground.

b. Slowly lower the weight back to its original starting position, the same way you brought it up.

Tip: All rotator cuff exercises should always be performed very slowly and smoothly, and the weights for these exercises should NEVER exceed three lbs. or injuries will occur.

Rotator Cuff on Side

Area trained: Rotator cuff.

Starting Position: Lie on your side on a bench with your upper arm resting on your chest, parallel to the floor, and bent at the elbow at a ninety-degree angle so that your hand is hanging. Hold a light weight in that hand.

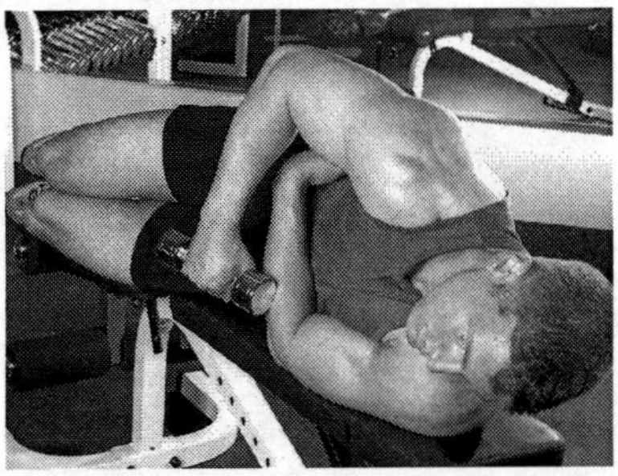

Lift:

a. Keeping everything else stationary, rotate your arm upward until it becomes parallel with the ground.

b. Slowly lower the weight back to its original starting position, the same way you brought it up.

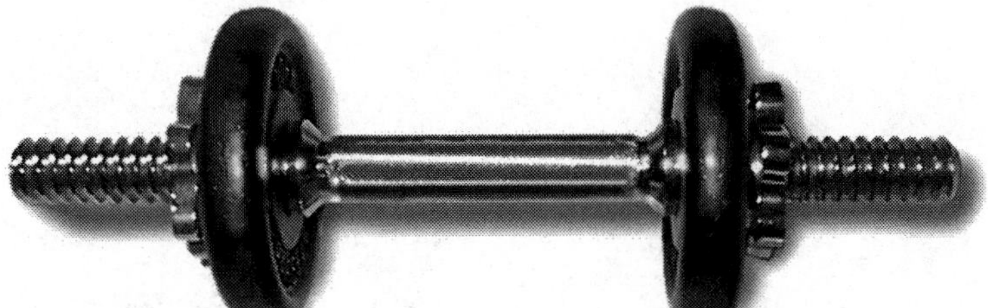

TRICEPS EXERCISES

Interchangeable Triceps Exercises

1 Triceps Push Downs

1 Triceps Pull Downs

1 Skull Crushers

1 Triceps Kickbacks

1 Bench Dips

2 Barbell Triceps Curls

2 Dumbbell Triceps Curls

2 One-Arm Triceps Extensions

Triceps Push Downs

Prime movers: Triceps.

Starting Position: Stand or kneel with your back straight in front of a cable machine. Grab the bar with an overhand grip. Keep your elbows tucked in at your sides and hold the bar up by your chin.

Lift:

a. Keeping your body still and elbows tucked at your sides, push the bar straight down until your arms are fully extended.

b. Come to a brief, complete stop before slowly allowing the bar to rise back up to the starting position, with your elbows remaining tucked at your sides at all time.

Tip: For variation, you can use many types of bars, including one-arm handles.

Triceps Pull Downs

This exercise is identical to triceps push downs with an underhand grip.

Skull Crushers

Prime movers: Triceps.

Starting Position: Lie on a bench with your head partially hanging off the end. Hold a barbell with a close overhand grip straight out in front of you, above your forehead, with your arms extended.

Lift:

a. Keeping your body still and elbows motionless, slowly lower your forearms and the barbell down behind your head as far as you can.

b. Come to a brief, complete stop before returning the barbell to the starting position the same way you brought it down. Keep your elbows in and do not use your shoulders.

Tip: If having your head partially off of the bench feels awkward and difficult, then perform this exercise with your head resting on the bench.

If balance becomes an issue while performing any cable machine triceps exercise, stand stagger stepped, with one leg behind the other.

Triceps Kickbacks

Prime movers: Triceps.

Starting Position: Stand bending at the waist so your upper body is parallel with the floor with your knees slightly bent. Stand stagger stepped or place one knee on a bench and place your opposite hand on a bench for balance. With your elbow tucked in at your side and your upper arm also parallel to the floor, let your lower arm hang down perpendicular to the floor.

Lift:

a. Keeping your body still and elbow motionless, raise your lower arm backward until your arm is fully extended.

b. Come to a brief, complete stop before slowly lowering the dumbbell to the starting position, the same way you brought it up. Keep your elbow in and do not use your shoulder.

Bench Dips

Prime movers: Triceps, shoulders.

Starting Position: Place your heels on one bench in front of you and your palms on another bench behind you shoulder-width, leaving your rear hanging in the air. Your heels should be together and your hands should be shoulder-width apart. Your arms should be extended so that your body is elevated.

Lift:

a. Slowly lower yourself by bending at the elbows as low as you can by keeping the elbows tucked in as much as possible and keeping your back straight.

b. Push yourself back up to full extension with your arms locked.

Tip: If your body weight alone is not providing enough resistance for a good workout, try placing some weights on your lap.

Barbell Triceps Curls

Prime movers: Triceps.

Starting Position: Stand or sit upright and hold a barbell above your head with your arms locked out and your elbows close to your head.

Lift:

a. Keeping your body still and elbows fixed close to your head, slowly lower your forearms and the bar down behind your head as far as you can.

b. Come to a brief, complete stop before returning the bar to the starting position, the same way you brought it down. Keep your elbows in and do not use your shoulders.

Tip: Keeping your elbows in close to your head is sometimes difficult to do, but it ensures the best triceps workout.

Dumbbell Triceps Curls

Prime movers: Triceps.

Starting Position: Stand or sit upright and hold a dumbbell above your head with both hands, your arms locked out, and your elbows close to your head.

Lift:

a. Keeping your body still and elbows fixed close to your head, slowly lower your forearms and the dumbbell down as far as you can.

b. Come to a brief, complete stop before returning the dumbbell to the starting position, the same way you brought it down. Keep your elbows in and do not use your shoulders.

One-Arm Triceps Extensions

Prime movers: Triceps.

Starting Position: Stand or sit upright and hold a dumbbell above your head with one hand. Keep your arm locked out and your elbow close to your head.

Lift:

a. Keeping your body still and elbow fixed close to your head, slowly lower your forearm and the dumbbell down behind your head as far as you can.

b. Come to a brief, complete stop before returning the dumbbell to the starting position, the same way you brought it down. Keep your elbow in and do not use your shoulder.

Biceps/Forearms Exercises

Interchangeable Biceps/ Forearms Exercises

1 Barbell Curls

1 Dumbbell Curls

1 Preacher Curls

1 Incline Dumbbell Curls

1 Concentration Curls

2 Reverse Barbell Curls

2 Reverse Dumbbell Curls

2 Hammer Curls

3 Behind Back Wrist Curls

3 Reverse Wrist Curls

Barbell Curls

Prime movers: Biceps.

Starting Position: Stand upright with your feet roughly shoulder-width apart. Hold a barbell with your palms facing away from your body and elbows tucked into your sides.

Lift:

a. Keeping your elbows tucked at your sides at all times, use your biceps to curl the bar upward as high as you can until it is just below your chin.

b. With your elbows still tucked at your sides, slowly lower the bar back to its original starting position.

Tip: Performing cheat curls (allowing your body to rock backward slightly to gain momentum) with this exercise from time to time can be beneficial to gaining mass in the biceps. You MUST wear a weight-lifting belt if you perform cheat curls.

Dumbbell Curls

Prime movers: Biceps.

Starting Position: Stand or sit upright and with your feet roughly shoulder-width apart, hold dumbbells with your palms facing away from your body and elbows tucked into your sides.

Lift:

a. Keeping your elbows tucked at your sides at all times, use your biceps to curl the dumbbells upward as high as you can. You can curl with both arms at the same time or alternate arms.

b. With your elbows still tucked at your sides, slowly lower the bar back to its original starting position.

Tip for all dumbbell biceps exercises:
Rotating your wrists inward towards your body will add extra emphasis and will give your biceps an even greater peak.

Preacher Curls

Prime movers: Biceps.

Starting Position: Sit at a preacher bench with your elbows resting on the bench shoulder-width apart. Grip the bar with your palms facing upward.

Lift:

a. With your elbows remaining stationary, use your biceps to curl the bar upward as high as you can towards your chin, where you should flex your biceps for extra emphasis.

b. Slowly lower the bar back to its original starting point with your arms fully extended.

Tip: A closer grip trains your outer biceps and a wider grip trains your inner biceps.

Incline Dumbbell Curls

Prime movers: Biceps.

Starting Position: Sit on an inclined bench with your elbows tucked at your sides and your arms fully extended. Grip the dumbbells with your palms facing upward.

Lift:

a. Keeping your elbows tucked at your sides at all times, use your biceps to curl the dumbbells upward as high as you can. You can curl with both arms at the same time or alternate arms.

b. With your elbows still tucked at your sides, slowly lower the bar back to its original starting position.

Concentration Curls

Prime movers: Biceps.

Starting Position: Sit on a bench slightly bent forward with your left arm gripping a dumbbell hanging between your legs. Your left palm should face your right leg and your right arm should rest on your knee.

Lift:

a. Keeping your elbow and upper arm stationary, curl the weight upward towards your shoulder.

b. With your elbow and upper arm still stationary, slowly lower the bar back to its original starting position.

Reverse Barbell Curls

Prime movers: Forearms, biceps.

Starting Position: Stand upright with your feet roughly shoulder-width apart. Hold a barbell with your palms towards your body, your wrists locked, and elbows tucked into your sides.

Lift:

a. Keeping your elbows tucked at your sides and wrists locked at all times, use your forearms and biceps to curl the bar upward as high as you can or until it is just below your chin.

b. With your elbows still tucked at your sides, slowly lower the bar back to its original starting position.

Tip: Keeping your wrists locked adds extra emphasis to your forearms and ensures a great workout.

Reverse Dumbbell Curls

Prime movers: Forearms, biceps.

Starting Position: Stand or sit upright with your feet roughly shoulder-width apart. Hold two dumbbells with your palms facing towards your body, your wrists locked, and elbows tucked into your sides.

Lift:

a. Keeping your elbows tucked at your sides and wrists locked at all times, use your forearms and biceps to curl the dumbbells upward as high as you can. You can curl with both arms at the same time or alternate arms.

b. With your elbows still tucked at your sides and wrists locked, slowly lower the bar back to its original starting position.

Hammer Curls

Prime movers: Forearms, biceps.

Starting Position: Stand or sit upright with your feet roughly shoulder-width apart. Hold two dumbbells with your palms facing each other, your wrists locked, and elbows tucked into your sides.

Lift:

a. Keeping your elbows tucked at your sides, wrists locked, and palms facing each other at all times, use your forearms and biceps to curl the dumbbells upward as high as you can. You can curl with both arms at the same time or alternate arms.

b. With your elbows still tucked at your sides, wrists locked, and palms facing each other, slowly lower the dumbbells back to their original starting position.

Behind Back Wrist Curls

Prime movers: Forearms.

Starting Position: Stand upright with your feet roughly shoulder-width apart. Hold a barbell behind your back as if you are handcuffed with your palms facing away from your body and elbows tucked into your sides.

Lift:

a. Keeping your elbows tucked at your sides at all times, use your wrists to curl the bar upward towards your forearms.

b. With your elbows still tucked at your sides, slowly lower the bar with your wrists back to its original starting position.

Reverse Wrist Curls

Prime movers: Forearms.

Starting Position: Sit at the end of a bench. Hold a barbell with an overhand grip with your palms facing the floor and your forearms resting on your thighs.

Lift:

a. Keeping everything stationary, use your wrists to curl the bar backwards as far as you can.

b. Slowly lower the bar with your wrists, back to its original starting position.

Legs Exercises

Interchangeable Leg Exercises

1 Squats

1 Leg Press

1 Dead Lift

1 Leg Extensions

1 Leg Curls

2 Standing Calf Raises

2 Seated Calf Raises

2 Reverse Calf Raises

3 Jump Squats

3 Power Cleans

4 Box Steps

4 Lunges

Squats

Prime movers: Upper and lower legs.

Starting Position: Stand upright with your feet shoulder-width apart and a barbell resting behind your neck on your traps with your hands slightly wider than shoulder-width apart, using an overhand grip. Keep your back straight and your head tilted up.

Lift:

a. With your back remaining straight and your head tilted up, slowly lower the weight by bending your knees until the upper part of your legs is parallel with the floor.

b. Explode upward back to the starting position. The entire lift should be in one smooth, fluid motion.

Tip for squats and dead lifts: Standing up on your toes as high as you can and holding it for a second or so upon returning to the starting position is a great built-in calves workout.

Leg Press

Prime movers: Upper and lower legs.

Starting Position: Sit in a leg press machine with your back straight. Place your hands on the handlebars and your feet on the support bar.

Lift:

a. With everything remaining still, slowly lower the weight by bending your knees as far as you can.

b. Explode upward back to the starting position. The entire lift should be in one smooth, fluid motion.

Tip: By not lowering the weights down very far, you are able to lift more weights, but will not be training your legs through the entire range of motion.

Dead Lift:

Prime movers: Upper and lower legs.

Starting Position: Stand with your back straight, head tilted back, and leaning slightly forward at the waist. Bend your knees so you can grab a barbell with your arms fully extended.

a. Keeping your arms locked, push with your legs to an upright position. Your lower back will also be used, but try to concentrate on using only your legs to lift the bar off the floor.

b. Slowly lower the bar so that it comes a few inches from the floor, with your arms and back remaining straight and head tilted up.

Tip: You may find this exercise easier to perform by gripping the bar with one hand using an overhand grip and the other hand using an underhand grip as shown in the pictures.

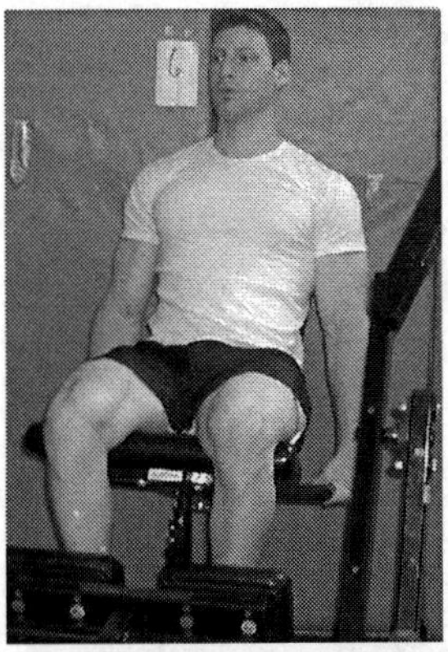

Leg Extensions

Prime movers: Upper legs.

Starting Position: Sit with your back straight and hands gripping the handlebars in a leg-extension machine. Place your feet underneath the bar.

Lift:

a. With everything remaining still, raise the bar with your feet by extending your legs as far as you can.

b. Slowly lower your legs back down towards the starting position the same way you brought them up.

Tip: If all of the weights on your leg extension/curl machine are still not enough for you, you can perform this exercise one leg at a time.

Leg Curls

Prime movers: Hamstrings

Starting Position: With your back straight and hands gripping the handlebars, lie face down on a leg curl machine and place your feet underneath the bar.

Lift:

a. With everything remaining still, raise the bar with your feet by curling your legs as far as you can.

b. Slowly lower your legs towards the starting position the same way you brought them up.

Standing Calf Raises

Prime movers: Calves.

Starting Position: Stand with your shoulders under the supports of a standing calf raise machine and your toes on the elevated stand provided so that your heels are hanging off the end. Keep your back straight and hands gripping the handlebars.

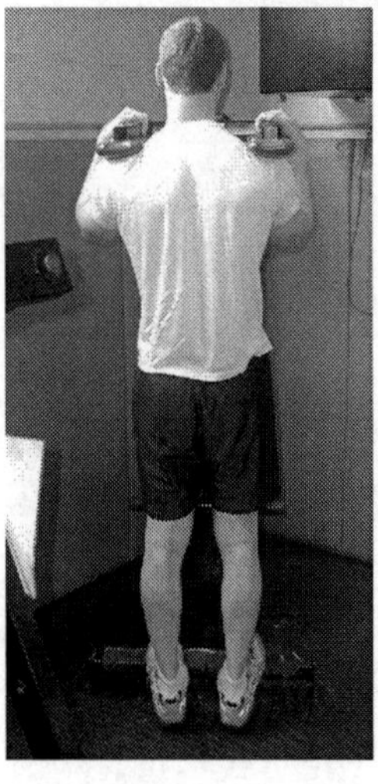

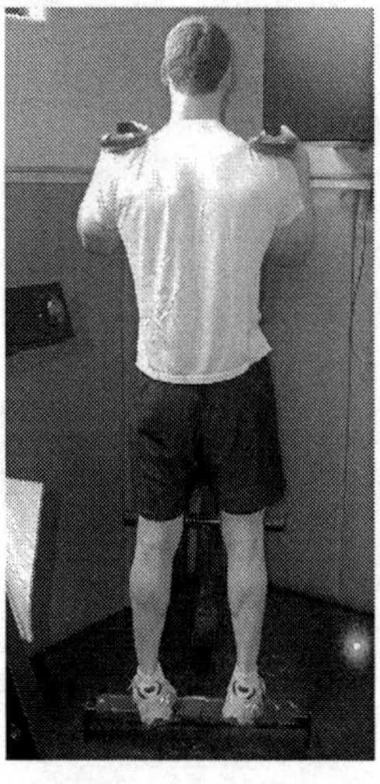

a. With everything remaining still, stand up on your toes as high as you can Hold the position for a brief moment to maximize the work on your calves.

b. Slowly lower your heels back down towards the starting position the same way you brought them up.

Tip for all calf raises: To ensure the best workout, raise and lower your heels as high and as low as you can, training your calves through the entire range of motion.

Seated Calf Raises

Prime movers: Calves.

Starting Position: Sit with your knees under the supports of a standing calf raise machine and your toes on the elevated stand provided so that your heels are hanging off of the stand. Keep your back straight and hands gripping the handlebars.

a. With everything remaining still, rise up on your toes as high as you can. Hold the position for a brief moment to maximize the work on your calves.

b. Slowly lower your heels back down towards the starting position the same way you brought them up.

Reverse Calf Raises

Prime movers: Front of lower legs.

Starting Position: Stand upright with your heels on an elevated stand or block so that your toes are hanging off the stand. This exercise is best performed with no added resistance other than your body weight.

a. With everything remaining still, stand up on your heels as high as you can. Hold the position for a brief moment to maximize the work on the front of your lower legs.

b. Slowly lower your toes back down towards the starting position the same way you brought them up.

Jump Squats

Prime movers: Upper and lower legs.

Starting Position: Stand in a squatting position with your feet shoulder-width apart and your arms crossed over your chest. Keep your back straight and your head tilted up.

Lift:

a. With everything remaining still, explosively jump straight up as high as you can.

b. As you land, return to the starting position in one smooth motion.

Power Cleans

Prime movers: Upper and lower legs.

Starting Position: Stand with your back straight and head titled back. Lean slightly forward at the waist so your shoulders are in front of the bar on the floor. Keep your feet at least shoulder-width apart and your knees bent so you can grab a barbell with your arms fully extended, using an overhand grip.

a. Keeping your arms straight, push with your legs and raise the bar up close to your body to your lower thigh with your knees still slightly bent.

b. From this point, use your lower body for momentum to push yourself straight up while simultaneously using your shoulders to raise the bar to your stomach.

c. In one explosive movement, flip your wrists and elbows underneath the bar while simultaneously jumping into a partial squatting position.

Box Steps

Prime movers: Upper and lower legs.

Starting Position: Stand upright with your feet shoulder-width apart and a barbell resting behind your neck on your traps with your hands slightly wider than shoulder-width apart, using an overhand grip or holding dumbbells at your sides. Keep your back straight and your head tilted up. Stand with a box, bench, or some sort of elevated apparatus in front of you.

a. Step forward up on the box or bench with your right foot. Bring your left knee up so that your left thigh is parallel to the floor.

b. Lower your left leg all the way back down to the floor and bring your right leg back down to meet it. Repeat with other leg.

Lunges

Prime movers: Upper and lower legs.

Starting Position: Stand upright with your feet together and either a barbell resting behind your neck on your traps or holding two dumbbells at your sides as in the picture. Your hands should be slightly wider than shoulder-width apart, using an overhand grip. Keep your back straight and your head tilted up.

Lift:

a. With everything remaining still, slowly take a large step forward with one leg, bending both knees. The weight on your back foot should come up on your toes, and the knee on your back leg should come very close, but not touch the floor.

b. Using your extended leg, thrust yourself back to the starting position the same way you came down. The entire lift should be in one smooth, fluid motion.

Tip: The longer your step forward, the more effective this exercise will be.

Part IV

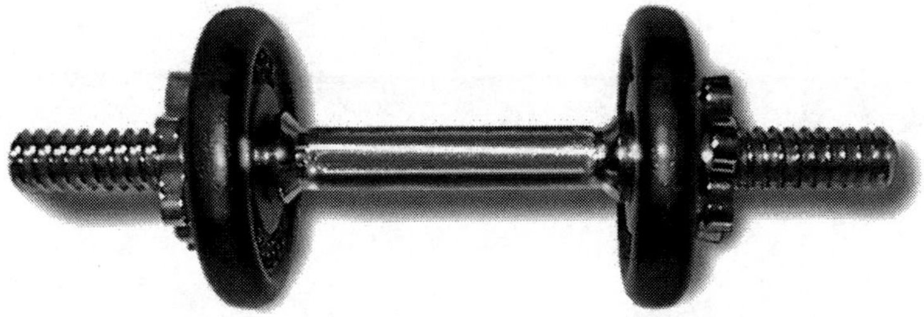

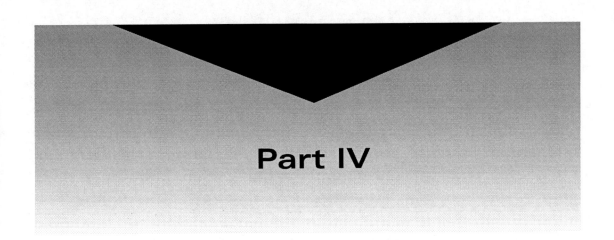

The Necessities

Perfecting Your Technique

This section identifies what you need to accomplish before you begin any one of the programs. The information in this section is extremely important for beginners and is also important for experienced weight trainers who have never performed some of the recommended exercises. To follow any type of weight-training routine, you first need to get a feel for the weight room and learn your own strengths.

Now is the time to test out your form, style, and technique. After you have picked the program you would like to follow, be sure to take a day or so to perform warm-up sets with each of the exercises listed in that specific program. The object of these first few sessions is not to train so hard that you are sore the following days, but to practice your form and to gain an understanding for yourself and for the weight room. Simply go to the gym with this book, read the recommended exercises section, and go through a few reps of each exercise using very light weights.

These initial days of practice are very important and can be a major help to you as you progress as a weight trainer and athlete by helping you gain an understanding of approximately how much weight you can handle for each exercise.

Estimating Your One Rep Max

Tip

Your one rep max *is the greatest amount of weight you can lift at one time or for one repetition for a particular exercise.*

Knowing your one rep max is an essential part of measuring your strength, your progress, and is very helpful in determining the weight load you should be lifting for every set, regardless of your purpose. This section is called *Estimating* Your One Rep Max because this book never recommends that you *max out*. As discussed in earlier sections, *maxing out* can cause injuries, which, besides being painful and dangerous, can prevent future weight training. *Auxiliary exercises,* or exercises training smaller muscle groups such as biceps and forearms, can be particularly dangerous when trying to max out. With the estimated one rep max chart provided for you, you can estimate your one rep max without having to attempt to lift your max weight. Instead, you can lift a lighter weight several times to safely and accurately estimate what your max is.

Your estimated one rep max for each exercise in an underlying foundation for this book. You will see once you've read through the rest of the text that all of the sets and reps you are required to perform are based on percentages of your estimated one rep max. Depending on your goals, you will be required to lift different percentages of your estimated one rep max.

Understanding the Chart

Steps to finding your estimated one rep max:

1. Choose an exercise that you want to try to find your estimated one rep max.

2. Choose a test weight that is light enough for you to lift several, but not more than, eight times.

3. Lift that weight until failure. If you lift more than eight reps, choose a higher weight and start over.

4. Find your test weight on the far left column of the Estimated One-Rep Max Chart.

5. Find the number of reps you successfully completed on the top row.

6. Scroll right from your test weight and down from your successfully completed reps until you find the number that shares both the same row and column.

The number you arrive at is your estimated one rep max.

REPS

WEIGHT

	1	2	3	4	5	6	7	8
5	5	5	5	6	6	6	6	6
10	10	10	11	11	11	12	12	12
15	15	15	16	16	17	17	18	19
20	20	21	21	22	23	23	24	25
25	25	26	27	27	28	29	30	31
30	30	31	32	33	34	35	36	37
35	35	36	37	38	39	41	42	44
40	40	41	42	44	45	47	48	50
45	45	46	48	49	51	52	54	56
50	50	51	53	55	56	58	60	62
55	55	57	58	60	62	64	66	68
60	60	62	64	66	68	70	72	75
65	65	67	69	71	73	76	78	81
70	70	72	74	76	79	81	84	87
75	75	77	79	82	84	87	90	93
80	80	82	85	87	90	93	96	99
85	85	87	90	93	96	99	102	106
90	90	93	95	98	101	105	108	112
95	95	98	101	104	107	110	114	118
100	100	103	106	109	113	116	120	124
105	105	108	111	115	118	122	126	130
110	110	113	117	120	124	128	132	137
115	115	118	122	126	129	134	138	143
120	120	123	127	131	135	139	144	149

REPS

WEIGHT

	1	2	3	4	5	6	7	8
125	125	129	132	136	141	145	150	155
130	130	134	138	142	146	151	156	161
135	135	139	143	147	152	157	162	168
140	140	144	148	153	158	163	168	174
145	145	149	154	158	163	168	174	180
150	150	154	159	164	169	174	180	186
155	155	159	164	169	174	180	186	193
160	160	165	169	175	180	186	192	199
165	165	170	175	180	186	192	198	205
170	170	175	180	186	191	197	204	211
175	175	180	185	191	197	203	210	217
180	180	185	191	196	203	209	216	224
185	185	190	196	202	208	215	222	230
190	190	195	201	207	214	221	228	236
195	195	201	207	213	219	227	234	242
200	200	206	212	218	225	232	240	248
205	205	211	217	224	231	238	246	255
210	210	216	222	229	236	244	252	261
215	215	221	228	235	242	250	258	267
220	220	226	233	240	248	256	264	273
225	225	231	238	246	253	261	270	279
230	230	237	244	251	259	267	276	286
235	235	242	249	256	264	273	282	292
240	240	247	254	262	270	279	288	298

REPS

WEIGHT

	1	2	3	4	5	6	7	8
245	245	252	259	267	276	285	294	304
250	250	257	265	273	281	290	300	310
255	255	262	270	278	287	296	306	317
260	260	267	275	284	293	302	312	323
265	265	273	281	289	298	308	318	329
270	270	278	286	295	304	314	324	335
275	275	283	291	300	309	319	330	341
280	280	288	297	306	315	325	336	348
285	285	293	302	311	321	331	342	354
290	290	298	307	316	326	337	348	360
295	295	303	312	322	332	343	354	366
300	300	309	318	327	338	348	360	373
305	305	314	323	333	343	354	366	379
310	310	319	328	338	349	360	372	385
315	315	324	334	344	354	366	378	391
320	320	329	339	349	360	372	384	397
325	325	334	344	355	366	378	390	404
330	330	339	349	360	371	383	396	410
335	335	345	355	366	377	389	402	416
340	340	350	360	371	383	395	408	422
345	345	355	365	376	388	401	414	428
350	350	360	371	382	394	407	420	435
355	355	365	376	387	399	412	426	441
360	360	370	381	393	405	418	432	447

REPS

WEIGHT

	1	2	3	4	5	6	7	8
365	365	375	387	398	411	424	438	453
370	370	381	392	404	416	430	444	459
375	375	386	397	409	422	436	450	466
380	380	391	402	415	428	441	456	472
385	385	396	408	420	433	447	462	478
390	390	401	413	426	439	453	468	484
395	395	406	418	431	444	459	474	490
400	400	411	424	436	450	465	480	497
405	405	417	429	442	456	470	486	503
410	410	422	434	447	461	476	492	509
415	415	427	439	453	467	482	498	515
420	420	432	445	458	473	488	504	522
425	425	437	450	464	478	494	510	528
430	430	442	455	469	484	499	516	534
435	435	447	461	475	489	505	522	540
440	440	453	466	480	495	511	528	546
445	445	458	471	486	501	517	534	553
450	450	463	477	491	506	523	540	559
455	455	468	482	496	512	529	546	565
460	460	473	487	502	518	534	552	571
465	465	478	492	507	523	540	558	577
470	470	483	498	513	529	546	564	584
475	475	489	503	518	534	552	570	590
480	480	494	508	524	540	558	576	596

REPS

WEIGHT

	1	2	3	4	5	6	7	8
485	485	499	514	529	546	563	582	602
490	490	504	519	535	551	569	588	608
495	495	509	524	540	557	575	594	615
500	500	514	529	546	563	581	600	621
505	505	519	535	551	568	587	606	627
510	510	525	540	556	574	592	612	633
515	515	530	545	562	579	598	618	639
520	520	535	551	567	585	604	624	646
525	525	540	556	573	591	610	630	652
530	530	545	561	578	596	616	636	658
535	535	550	567	584	602	621	642	664
540	540	555	572	589	608	627	648	671
545	545	561	577	595	613	633	654	677
550	550	566	582	600	619	639	660	683
555	555	571	588	606	624	645	666	689
560	560	576	593	611	630	650	672	695
565	565	581	598	616	636	656	678	702
570	570	586	604	622	641	662	684	708
575	575	591	609	627	647	668	690	714
580	580	597	614	633	653	674	696	720
585	585	602	619	638	658	679	702	726
590	590	607	625	644	664	685	708	733
595	595	612	630	649	669	691	714	739
600	600	617	635	655	675	697	720	745

The Different Folks, Different Strokes Principle

As the title of this section indicates, not everyone is the same. In weight training, differences can occur both physically and psychologically. Some people are born with greater muscle-building capabilities than others. A major reason for these genetic differences is the amount of fast-twitch muscle fibers one has. Fast-twitch fibers are able to grow bigger and stronger than the other muscle fibers. Do not feel frustrated if you see others making faster initial gains than you are, because you can and will make enormous gains by following any one of the provided programs. By sticking with your routine and working hard, you can catch and surpass almost everyone. Fast-twitch, as well as slow-twitch fibers, are explained in further detail in the section *Muscle Fibers*.

Weight trainers also differ mentally and psychologically. Different people have different preferences in terms of how they like to work out, what exercises they like to do, as well as how often they like to train. Many of the various programs in this book are based on contrasting styles of equally legitimate training principles. Some programs are for strength and bulk building, others for power enhancement, and still others for increasing endurance, stamina, and burning fat.

Overtraining *is when you work out so hard that your training negatively affects your goals.*

Overtraining and Staleness

Your muscles need at least forty-eight hours to fully recover from weight training, which is why you should never train the same muscle groups on consecutive days.

Everyone, at one point or another, reaches a plateau in his or her training. When this happens, gains are very hard to come by. Many times plateaus occur because of overtraining. Overtraining can occur during one workout, or it can gradually creep up on you over time. It is important to push yourself as hard as you can in the gym and make the most of your time, but there can be a time when you are doing too much. Training seven days a week is an example of overtraining. We all need rest days so our muscles can recoup, regroup, and rebuild. It is during these days off that your body is able to grow bigger and stronger. None of our programs requires you to lift all seven days of the week because it would not allow enough time for your muscles to fully recover. Even the biggest and strongest athletes, body builders, and weight lifters take at least one day of rest per week.

During one session, some people are able to work out for hours without overtraining, while others simply can't handle that much physical stress. Most beginners will not be able to work out for as long or as often as more experienced weight trainers because their bodies are not yet prepared for that type of strenuous work.

Staleness, on the other hand, is thought by many experts to be a response to overtraining. It is a syndrome that negatively affects your athletic performance and your personality. Rest is the only method of prevention and the only cure for staleness. The programs provided for you all have been designed so that there is a minimal chance of overtraining and staleness occurring; however, if you do begin to notice symptoms, take at least one week off from weight training and see your physician.

Symptoms of staleness include:

1. Reaching a plateau in training gains

2. Having unusual sleeping patterns

3. Performing tasks seems more difficult

4. Having a decreased appetite leading to unhealthy lean body weight loss

5. Having increased irritability and anxiety

6. Experiencing depression

7. Having a decreased sex drive

Endurance athletes are at the greatest risk of staleness; however, all athletes should be aware of this syndrome regardless of the sport. The different folks, different strokes principle applies to staleness. Many athletes may never experience staleness, but everyone needs to be aware that it can happen.

The Declaration of Variation

Variation is introducing some sort of change in your workout routine. It can be the constant changing of exercises within a program or the compete changing of your program every few weeks. Variation is very important in weight training for several physiological and psychological reasons. Some of the most important benefits of variation in a weight-training program include:

1. **Not allowing your body to adapt to any one routine:** Perhaps the most important reason to vary your routines is so you can keep making progress and gains. Variation is the key to continued progress. Your body is a machine designed to adapt to any stress placed on it, whether it be heat, pressure, or tension. Similarly, your body adapts to the workload you are putting on it in the gym. After following the same routine for long enough, you will plateau because your body has become used to and has adapted to doing the same thing over and over again. When a plateau occurs, you need to shock your body with different types of stimuli to continue making gains. By occasionally switching the type of training you do (how many reps, sets, exercises, and their order), you shock your body so that it has to readapt to the new workload you are putting on it, which enables you to continue to progress.

2. **Keeping you from getting bored:** Following the same routine day after day can become very boring and tiresome. Fitness experts and coaches alike know that boredom in the gym can be a major problem for athletes and other weight trainers. In order to make big gains, you need to train hard and with intensity. Once that intensity is lost, so are the benefits from training hard. When people are bored with their routine, they lose motivation and train with less passion. It is human nature. Unfortunately, this lack of motivation spawns a negative cycle. By not training as hard, gains become more difficult, thus leading to an even greater decrease in moti-

vation, which leads again to not training hard. And so the cycle continues. Varying exercises and styles every so often keeps things fresh and keeps people motivated, especially athletes in the midst of a long off-season. For these reasons, each of the programs in the back of the book last for only four weeks with slight changes occurring after two weeks.

3. **Targeting, strengthening, and toning every part of every muscle:** As you've noticed, this book provides you with many weight-training exercises. Many of these exercises train the same muscle groups. Like people, no two exercises are exactly alike. Some may be similar, but not identical. Each exercise targets your muscle from a different angle and achieves a different benefit. By using a variety of exercises on the same muscles, you strengthen every part of those muscles. It is the key to really defining your entire body, providing you with more explosive power for athletic events, and creating nice separation between muscle groups.

It is the idea of variation that makes this book what it is. Variation is the reason this book includes 54 different programs each designed for different purposes.

Muscle Fibers

(How to Train, What and Why)

Our muscles are made up of many bundles of muscle fibers. Each fiber type has its own characteristics and purposes. For simplicity purposes, these muscle fibers can be categorized as:

1. **Fast-Twitch Fibers**
2. **Slow-Twitch Fibers**
3. **Intermediate Fibers (properties of both)**

The muscle-fiber makeup in most people is roughly 25% fast twitch, 25% slow twitch, and 50% intermediate fibers, which contain properties of both fast- and slow-twitch muscle fibers. With proper training some of the intermediate fibers can be converted to fast- or slow–twitch fibers. The more fast-twitch fibers one has, the more powerful and explosive he or she will be. People with more slow-twitch fibers will have greater endurance and stamina. Depending on your purpose, you can weight train in order to build up either muscle fiber.

Fast-Twitch Fibers

Generally, fast-twitch fibers are used in strength and explosive sports or sports that require bursts of speed and power for relatively short amounts of time. A running back bursting through a hole, a baseball or softball player trying to beat out an infield hit, a basketball player exploding up to the hoop for a slam, a golfer ripping a drive three hundred yards off the tee, a tennis player smashing a backhand across the court, a short distance swimmer torpedoing through the water, and a 110 hurdler flying down the lane are all putting their fast-twitch fibers to the test. Any type of explosive movement is being performed by fast-twitch fibers. People who participate in these or similar types of activities should concentrate primarily on working their fast-twitch fibers

The simple reason more fast-twitch muscle fibers lead to better performance in explosive activities is because they contract faster and with more power than slow-twitch fibers. Fast-twitch fibers lead to ***hypertrophy***—an increase in the size of muscle fibers as an outcome of weight training—more easily than slow-twitch fibers. As your muscle fibers increase in size, so do your muscles. The downside to fast-twitch fibers is that they can only work at full capacity for short periods of time before fatiguing because they work primarily without oxygen, or ***anaerobically***, and get most of their energy from limited stores of muscle glycogen.

Slow-Twitch Fibers

Slow-twitch fibers are used in stamina and endurance-based activities. Long distance runners, cyclists, swimmers, and triathletes are examples of people who should concentrate on slow-twitch training. Slow-twitch fibers contract more slowly than fast-twitch fibers, but are able to work for hours longer if trained properly. Slow-twitch fibers get their energy aerobically, from oxygen. Slow-twitch training is great for burning fat because oxygen stimulates the use of fat for energy. There is less hypertrophy in slow-twitch fibers, which is why marathon runners tend to be much smaller than football players.

TRAINING TECHNIQUES

Training to Failure:

Training to failure means training in a particular set until you exhaust yourself and cannot complete another repetition on your own. Whether you are training for endurance, power, or strength, it is recommended that you train to failure in most of your sets. By training to failure, you train your body to its maximum capabilities. This type of training is tough, but well worth the results.

Forced Reps:

Forced reps are performed directly after you have trained to positive failure and cannot complete another repetition. You lower the weight regularly and your partner helps you slowly lift it back up. Your partner should assist you to complete the rep, but not do all of the work for you. Your partner should make sure you spend at least three or four seconds on the positive phase of the lift while assisting you.

Negatives:

Negatives are also performed directly after you have trained to failure. The opposite of forced reps, the eccentric, or lowering aspect of the lift, is extremely slow, and the concentric part of the lift is fast, with the help of your partner. It should take you approximately six or seven seconds to lower the weights with the help of your partner. At this point, with the help from a spotter, quickly return the weights to their starting position and repeat. Using negatives is the best method for increasing strength and size; however, they should not be used very often because they work your muscles so hard they need over a week in order to fully recover before performing them again.

> *You are able to perform negatives with weights higher than your one rep max because eccentrically you can l ift a great deal more than you can concentrically.*

Supersets:

This is a training method where you perform one set of two exercises sequentially without rest. For example, if you were to superset preacher curls with triceps curls, you would do one set of preachers and immediately after completion, do one set of triceps curls and then rest before repeating.

Tri Sets:

Same as Supersets but with three exercises instead of two.

Pre-exhaust:

This method is one of the most intense methods of weight training. It is a form of supersetting where you perform many reps of a single-joint exercise and immediately follow it up with a compound exercise training the same muscles. For example, if you were to pre-exhaust your shoulders, you would first perform many reps of light lateral raises and immediately follow it up with a military press.

Burnouts (stripping method):

This method is very popular and very effective. Directly after you complete a set working to failure, immediately lighten the load of the weights so you can continue to train without rest, and perform the next set to failure where you will again lighten the load and work to failure.

Pyramid Method:

The pyramid method is a great strength-building tactic. It is performed properly by decreasing the reps and increasing the weight with every set. An example would be performing five reps with 100 lbs. followed by three reps with 120 lbs. and one rep with 140 lbs.

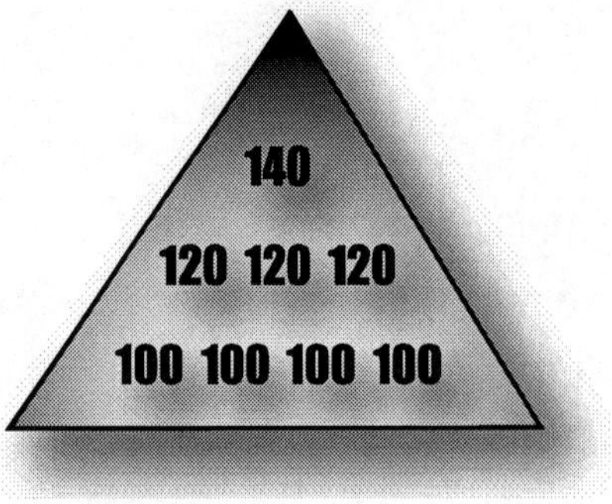

21s:

This method is most often performed for biceps exercises, particularly for preacher curls. These exercises are properly executed by performing seven reps going from the bottom of the lift to the halfway point and back for seven reps, then performing seven reps going from the halfway point to the top, followed by seven reps through the complete range of motion.

Cycling:

Cycling is rotating between two or three different routines. As long as the routines are different, it is considered cycling. A holistic cycle would be following an endurance program, then a power program, and then a strength program. It is best to take one week of active or complete rest after you have completed a full cycle to let your body completely recover before beginning again. Active rest is any sort of low-level, non-structured activity.

Circuit Training:

Circuit training is the best method of weight training for total fitness and aerobic benefits. It is a great way to get a fast and effective full-body workout. Circuit training is a type of endurance training in which you perform one set of six to ten exercises consecutively without rest. The six to ten exercises should train the major muscle groups of your entire body for a complete workout. After you have completed one circuit through the entire rotation, rest for a short time before repeating.

When to Increase

(The X + 3 Method)

Rule of Thumb: *Increase the number of reps before increasing the weight,*

The goal of weight training is to gradually increase the resistance over time. Two ways of increasing the resistance are:

1. Increasing the weight

2. Increasing the number of reps

Increasing the weight you lift can be overwhelming and difficult, so this book recommends that once a weight begins to feel too light for the designated number of repetitions, increase the number of reps before increasing the weight. The X + 3 method states that if you are required to lift X reps in a given set and are able to accomplish it, then the next time you lift, go for X + 1 reps using the same weight. As each exercise begins to feel lighter and lighter, increase your reps up until X + 3. When reps of X + 3 become easily attainable, increase the weight by 5 lbs. and return to reps of X, repeating this entire process. While training smaller, auxiliary-muscle groups like your biceps, triceps and forearms, make increases by 2 pounds at a time. Below is an example of the X + 3 method.

Your routine requires you to bench 100 lbs. 10 times. You complete the 10 reps with ease and the next time you go to the gym you lifts 100 lbs. 11 times. You continue this process until benching 100 lbs. 13 times becomes easy. At this point, you increase your bench to 105 lbs. and start back with 10 reps.

Choosing the Right Program

Provided for you are 54 programs/routines. Each one is designed for a different purpose. How do you know which one to choose? Below are important factors to consider when selecting your program:

Purpose:

The most important factor to consider when choosing your program is the purpose for which you are training. Do you want to get bigger, stronger, more toned, more powerful, leaner, or do you want to train for general fitness? If you want to get big and choose an endurance program, you will be working away from your goal. Make sure you choose a program that fits your purpose.

Weight-Training Experience:

The second factor to consider while choosing your program is your experience in the gym. For each style of training, you are offered different levels of intensity. If you are a beginner, you probably want to start out with a program of less time and frequency than the more advanced programs provided so you do not run the risk of overtraining. Likewise, if you are experienced in weight training and are looking to take the next step, you will most likely follow a program with more exercises and greater frequency to get a better workout.

Time Availability:

Your time availability is also a major factor in determining your program. You are provided with programs ranging from three to six days per week. For each style, you can choose between six levels of difficulty based on the amount of exercises and the frequency of your training. If you do not have much time to train, then choose a Level I or Level II program. If you have a lot of time to train and have the desire to train hard, then choose a Level IV or Level V program. Level VI programs are recommended only for the very advanced weight trainers. Assuming you train with the same intensity, you will see results faster by training with a more difficult program.

Personal Preference

This is the final element you should use while determining your program. The next section explains your choices.

Personal Preference

Once you have found all of the programs that meet your criteria in terms of purpose, experience, and time availability, you can make your final decision based on your personal preference. Take a look at each of the programs and decide which style of training you like more. You can choose between training *antagonistic* (opposite) muscle groups or *synergistic* (goal-congruent) muscle groups on the same day. These are the two major styles of weight training. Both are excellent ways of working out and are used equally by numerous athletes, body builders, and weight lifters. The styles are:

Antagonistic (Opposite) Muscle Training

Pros: By training antagonistic muscle groups on the same day, you are stretching your muscles and increasing your flexibility and range of motion. For example, while training your triceps, you are extending your arm, which stretches your biceps. You can become very flexible by using this style of training and stretching during your cooling down period.

Examples of antagonistic-muscle groups include:

Biceps/Triceps

Chest/Lats (Back)

Hamstrings/Quadriceps (thighs)

Abdominals/Lower Back

Cons: The major problem that arises from this style of training is fatigue. The larger the muscle group you are training, the more fatigued you will become. When training antagonistic muscle groups, you will train your chest and your lats (back) on the same day. These are both very large muscle groups, and, if you are training hard, you may experience some fatigue.

The larger the muscle group you are training, the more fatigued you will get.

Synergistic (Goal-Congruent) Muscle Training: "The Push-Pull Method"

Pros: Training synergistically allows you to train your muscles with even greater focus because every exercise you perform will be training at least one common muscle. Examples of synergistic training include training your chest and triceps on the same day because they both work out the triceps. Another example of this is working your lats (back) and your biceps, both training your biceps. This type of training is referred to as the ***push-pull method*** because you will be performing all of your pushing exercises on one day and all of your pulling exercises on the next.

Cons: The only true cost of training this way is that you do not get the stretch in your muscles during your weight-training session as you do in opposite-muscle training. If your sport requires serious flexibility, you may be better off training with the antagonistic muscle approach.

It is best if you periodically switch from one style to the next to shock your body with a different type of training. Try out both of the major styles of training and determine for yourself what works best for you.

Program Levels

All of the programs are broken down into six levels of difficulty. The least intense programs are Level I for beginners or for people without much time to spend in the gym. The most intense programs are Level VI, which are to be used exclusively by experienced weight trainers looking to take their training to the next stage. The Level I programs have been created to be easier on your body while still allowing you to make progress, and the Level VI programs have been created to train you as hard as possible without overtraining. The more intense the program, the faster you will see results.

Level I: Beginners

Level II: Somewhat intense

Level III: Moderate intensity

Level IV: Above average intensity

Level V: Very intense

Level VI: Extremely Intense — Recommended only for experienced weight trainers.

The program levels are not based on how hard you train while in the gym. The levels are based on three other factors:

1. **Frequency**
2. **Time**
3. **Advanced training methods**

Frequency: The programs provided for you are either three or four days per week, allowing you to increase them up to six days per week—except strength-training programs, which must not exceed five days per week. Therefore, the more frequent the program has you working out, the greater the total intensity of the program.

Three-days–a-week programs: Our least frequent programs require you to train three days per week. Anything less would not be enough training for you to make gains. Training twice a week is considered to be *maintenance training*, allowing you to do nothing more than maintain the gains you have already made.

Each one of the three-days-a-week programs trains your entire body in one session and can be performed by circuit training if you desire. Circuit training is explained in more detail in *Training Techniques*. Because you are training your entire body in one session, you are not able to put much focus on any one muscle group. Training a minimum of three days a week ensures that you are working every muscle in your body the required number of times per week to continue making gains. Also, because you are training your entire body during one session, the following day is always a rest day, providing your muscles with sufficient time to recoup and regroup.

Four-plus-days-a-week programs: As the frequency of the program grows, so do the choices. When you train more than three days per week, you cannot train your entire body in one single day because you would not be able to take a day of rest after every training session. With these more frequent programs, you can choose whether you want to follow a two- or three-day split. Training different muscle groups each day gives your muscles time to rest while other muscles are being trained, enabling you to train in consecutive days. Notice that you are never required to train all seven days of the week because your body needs at least one full day of rest to heal and grow stronger.

If you choose to increase the frequency of your prescribed program, bump up its level of difficulty by one.

Time: Certain programs contain more exercises than others. The number of required exercises relates directly to the time you will be spending in the gym. The more exercises the program has, the higher the intensity level will be.

Advanced-training methods: The last factor determining the level of the program is the use of advanced-training methods. These methods include negatives, supersets, forced reps, pre-exhausts, and burnouts, which are explained in further detail in the next section.

Tip

These methods are optional throughout each program. The use of advanced training methods moves the difficulty of the program up one level.

These methods are optional throughout each program. The use of advanced training methods moves the difficulty of the program up one level.

Each of the programs is designed for you to make serious gains and positive changes to your body, mind, health, and athletic ability. The more intense the program, the quicker you will be able to achieve and surpass your goals. The harder you train, the faster your muscles will respond. These programs have been carefully created so that you do not over- or undertrain yourself based on principles regarding sufficient time to rest and train your muscles.

Safety Reminders

When done properly, weight training can be a very effective way to sculpt your body and achieve your athletic potential. On top of all of the performance-enhancing benefits to weight training, it also plays a major role in injury reduction, injury prevention, and injury rehabilitation. With stronger muscles supporting your bones, tendons, and ligaments, you will be much less injury prone and will able to perform most activities hard and strong all the time. However, if necessary safety precautions are not followed, injuries can result.

Listed below are a few safety reminders to help keep you injury free in the gym.

Always use a spotter: It does not matter how experienced you are or how light you think the weight is, you always need someone to spot you.

Use safety collars: Collars will prevent weights from tipping over during a lift, which can result in an injury to you or others.

Pick up weights properly: Most injuries in the weight room come from picking up and putting weights down improperly. To avoid chronic lower-back problems, be sure to bend at the knees and to keep your back straight every time you pick up or put down weights.

Drink enough water: Even if you are not thirsty, be sure to drink lots of water before and during your workout, especially if you anticipate a lot of perspiration. As you become dehydrated, your ability to perform work drops way off, which will limit your intensity and slow your progress.

Use proper form: Proper form will provide you with the best results and help keep you injury free.

Breathe correctly: It is very important to simply breathe while performing any exercise, inhaling on the negative part of the lift and exhaling on the positive part. Do not hold your breath!

Do not drop weights: Not only can this break the weights, but it can also be very dangerous for everyone in the gym. Always put the weights back in a controlled manner.

Dress properly: Gym shoes are a must; wearing inappropriate gym attire like sandals can results in injuries such as broken toes.

Use your head: If you begin to feel sick, queasy, light-headed, or if you experience joint or chest pains, stop your session and get yourself checked out immediately.

Consult your physician: It is required for everyone to check with his or her physician before beginning any one of the prescribed programs or before increasing the intensity to any of the programs.

Record Keeping

When following any type of program, it is vital that you keep daily records for many reasons. Five of the most important are:

1. **Knowing when to increase the weight or reps**
2. **Knowing where to start after taking time away from the gym**
3. **Observing your gains over time**
4. **Motivation**
5. **Detect overtraining**

You can keep records on any or all of a vast number of factors that may be important to your training or progress. You have been provided with an example of a record-keeping chart to help you monitor your progress. You can print an unlimited amount of these charts from www.sportsworkout.com/chart.htm. They have been made accessible so you can keep records in the very best and easiest way possible. To complement the record-keeping chart, there is a testing sheet, which can also be printed from the Web site at www.sportsworkout.com/test.htm. With the testing sheets, you will be able to use formulas to literally put your strength, power, endurance, and athletic ability to the test.

You can find well-designed printable record-keeping charts at **www.sportsworkout.com/chart.htm** *that are designed to work with any one of the provided routines, and testing sheets at* **www.sportsworkout.com/test.htm** *where you can test your progress in many fashions.*

When to increase: Keeping records of your daily activity in the gym will allow you to determine when you are ready to increase the workload and by how much. Without well-kept records, your attempts to intensify your weight-training regimen will be made with hit or miss tactics. These tactics are not efficient ways to make gains because you will waste time by approximating your weight-loads and you may not be pushing yourself hard enough with the proper resistance. With well-kept records, you will know exactly when you need to increase the load and by how much.

Where to start: At one point or another, there will be instances when you will be unable to make it to the gym for extended periods of time. It may be because you become ill, experience a death in the family, or go on a vacation. The bottom line is there may be a time when you will stop your program and need to re-enter it. By keeping records, you will know exactly where you left off. Because you have taken time away from lifting, however, you will need to slightly decrease the load from where you left off, but you will have your records as a measuring stick. This is a very important aspect to training. If you take an extended period of time away from lifting without maintaining records, you will have to go by memory, which will result in trial and error once again.

Observe your gains: It is very important to be able to observe your gains for several reasons. The most important is that with well-kept records, you will be able to see which parts of the body you have made improvements in and which parts still need work. The records give you a sense of what changes need to be made for your next program to make up for these differences. You will want to saturate your next program with more exercises that train the weaker areas of your body, and this information can only be known with well-kept records.

Motivation: On top of monitoring your progress in the gym, record keeping provides you with the motivation to continue working harder and making bigger gains. You will literally be able to see on paper how you have progressed over time, which will inspire you to want to train harder. When people have hard evidence that they are actually making gains in the gym, it motivates them to continue making those gains.

Overtraining: How are record keeping and overtraining related? Even if you do not feel overtrained, you will be able to clearly see if you are overtrained by looking at your records. If, over time, you notice decreases from one day to the next in your records, the culprit may be overtraining. Overtraining may not always be the reason, but it very well could be. Other reasons could be changes in your eating or sleeping pattern or illness. In any case, record keeping will help you determine what the problem may be and how you can fix it.

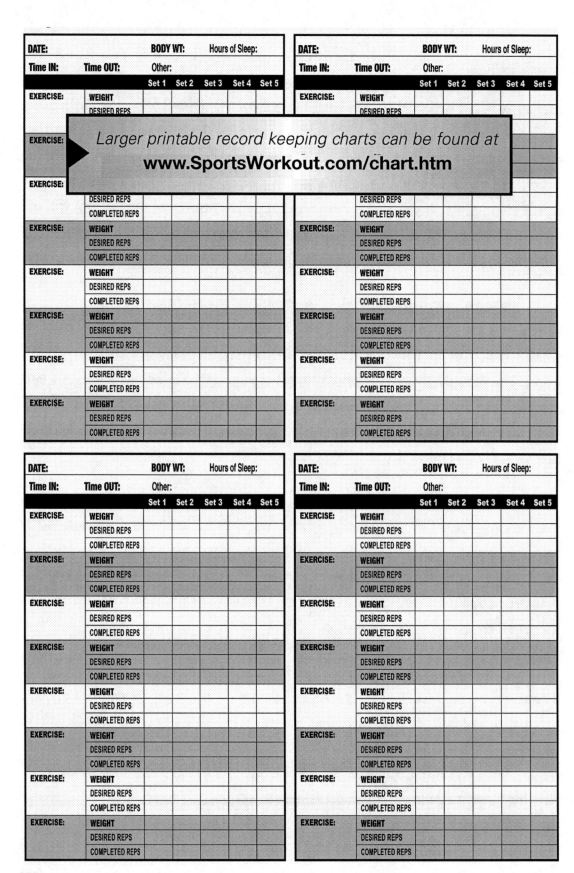

Larger printable record keeping charts can be found at

www.SportsWorkout.com/chart.htm

DATE: **BODY WT:** Hours of Sleep:

Time IN: **Time OUT:** Other:

		Set 1	Set 2	Set 3	Set 4	Set 5
EXERCISE:	WEIGHT					
	DESIRED REPS					
EXERCISE:						
EXERCISE:						
	DESIRED REPS					
	COMPLETED REPS					
EXERCISE:	WEIGHT					
	DESIRED REPS					
	COMPLETED REPS					
EXERCISE:	WEIGHT					
	DESIRED REPS					
	COMPLETED REPS					
EXERCISE:	WEIGHT					
	DESIRED REPS					
	COMPLETED REPS					
EXERCISE:	WEIGHT					
	DESIRED REPS					
	COMPLETED REPS					
EXERCISE:	WEIGHT					
	DESIRED REPS					
	COMPLETED REPS					

DATE: **BODY WT:** Hours of Sleep:

Time IN: **Time OUT:** Other:

		Set 1	Set 2	Set 3	Set 4	Set 5
EXERCISE:	WEIGHT					
	DESIRED REPS					
	DESIRED REPS					
	COMPLETED REPS					
EXERCISE:	WEIGHT					
	DESIRED REPS					
	COMPLETED REPS					
EXERCISE:	WEIGHT					
	DESIRED REPS					
	COMPLETED REPS					
EXERCISE:	WEIGHT					
	DESIRED REPS					
	COMPLETED REPS					
EXERCISE:	WEIGHT					
	DESIRED REPS					
	COMPLETED REPS					
EXERCISE:	WEIGHT					
	DESIRED REPS					
	COMPLETED REPS					

DATE: **BODY WT:** Hours of Sleep:

Time IN: **Time OUT:** Other:

		Set 1	Set 2	Set 3	Set 4	Set 5
EXERCISE:	WEIGHT					
	DESIRED REPS					
	COMPLETED REPS					
EXERCISE:	WEIGHT					
	DESIRED REPS					
	COMPLETED REPS					
EXERCISE:	WEIGHT					
	DESIRED REPS					
	COMPLETED REPS					
EXERCISE:	WEIGHT					
	DESIRED REPS					
	COMPLETED REPS					
EXERCISE:	WEIGHT					
	DESIRED REPS					
	COMPLETED REPS					
EXERCISE:	WEIGHT					
	DESIRED REPS					
	COMPLETED REPS					
EXERCISE:	WEIGHT					
	DESIRED REPS					
	COMPLETED REPS					
EXERCISE:	WEIGHT					
	DESIRED REPS					
	COMPLETED REPS					

DATE: **BODY WT:** Hours of Sleep:

Time IN: **Time OUT:** Other:

		Set 1	Set 2	Set 3	Set 4	Set 5
EXERCISE:	WEIGHT					
	DESIRED REPS					
	COMPLETED REPS					
EXERCISE:	WEIGHT					
	DESIRED REPS					
	COMPLETED REPS					
EXERCISE:	WEIGHT					
	DESIRED REPS					
	COMPLETED REPS					
EXERCISE:	WEIGHT					
	DESIRED REPS					
	COMPLETED REPS					
EXERCISE:	WEIGHT					
	DESIRED REPS					
	COMPLETED REPS					
EXERCISE:	WEIGHT					
	DESIRED REPS					
	COMPLETED REPS					
EXERCISE:	WEIGHT					
	DESIRED REPS					
	COMPLETED REPS					
EXERCISE:	WEIGHT					
	DESIRED REPS					
	COMPLETED REPS					

Test Yourself!

By testing yourself, you can visually see the gains you have made, and how extensive they have been. Provided for you at **www.sportsworkout.com/test.htm** are strength, power, endurance, and sport-specific tests so you can measure your progress in every fashion. You can also keep track of other important variables such as body weight, as well as muscle and waistline measurements.

> ▶ *Retest yourself every six weeks to monitor your gains.*

You can apply the strength, power, or endurance tests to any and all of the recommended exercises. However, it is suggested that you only test yourself in the bench press, leg press, military press, and lat pull because it would take days for you to test yourself in each of the recommended exercises. These four exercises are good indications of your overall fitness because they cover all of your major muscle groups. The bench press works your chest and triceps. The leg press covers your entire lower body. The lat pull has you working your lats and biceps. And military press trains your shoulders and traps.

The website provides you with several ways of testing yourself so that you will know exactly what you have improved in and what you may still need work on. For every non-weight-training related test, take the best of three tests to ensure the most accurate results.

Conclusion

You are now ready to begin weight training. You have all of the information in front of you and expert-designed programs for your use, equipping you with the best methods available to improve your athletic potential. You also know how to apply the exercises properly. With hard work and determination, you will achieve any goals you set for yourself. Best of luck training.

To further maximize your training, be sure to sign up for our Sport-Specific e-Training Program by going to www. SportsWorkout.com for one-on-one online training and customized workouts from personal trainers.

Part V

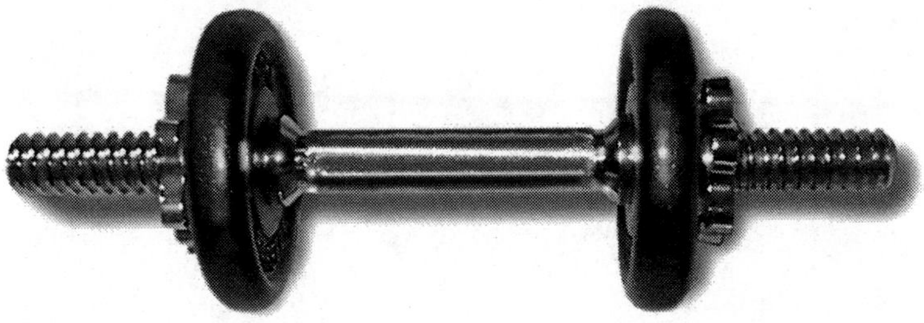

Supplemental 4-Week Programs

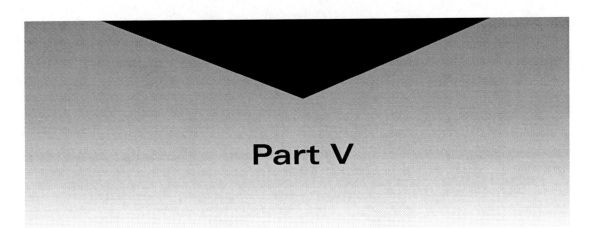

Endurance/ Fat Burning Training

Program Level I
Endurance/Fat Burning Training
Entire body every training day
Rest every other day

Weeks 1 and 2

Day 1

exercise	sets	reps
barbell bench press	3	20
seated cable rows	3	20
squats	3	20
dumbbell military press	3	20

Day 2

exercise	sets	reps
incline barbell bench press	3	20
one arm dumbbell rows	3	20
leg press	3	20
barbell military press	3	20

Day 3

exercise	sets	reps
barbell bench press	3	20
seated cable rows	3	20
squats	3	20
dumbbell military press	3	20

Weeks 3 and 4

Day 1

exercise	sets	reps
barbell bench press	3	25
seated cable rows	3	25
squats	3	25
dumbbell military press	3	25

Day 2

exercise	sets	reps
incline barbell bench press	3	25
one arm dumbbell rows	3	25
leg press	3	25
barbell military press	3	25

Day 3

exercise	sets	reps
barbell bench press	3	25
seated cable rows	3	25
squats	3	25
dumbbell military press	3	25

Program Level II
Endurance/Fat Burning Training
Entire body every training day
Rest every other day

Weeks 1 and 2

Day 1

exercise	sets	reps
barbell bench press	3	20
seated cable rows	3	20
squats	3	20
dumbbell military press	3	20
lunges	3	20
front raises	2	20

Day 2

exercise	sets	reps
dumbbell bench press	3	20
standing flyes	3	20
bent-over barbell rows	3	20
leg curls	3	20
standing calf raises	3	20
cable crossovers	2	20

Day 3

exercise	sets	reps
barbell bench press	3	20
seated cable rows	3	20
squats	3	20
dumbbell military press	3	20
lunges	3	20
front raises	2	20

Weeks 3 and 4

Day 1

exercise	sets	reps
barbell bench press	3	25
seated cable rows	3	25
squats	3	25
dumbbell military press	3	25
lunges	3	25
front raises	2	25

Day 2

exercise	sets	reps
dumbbell bench press	3	25
standing flyes	3	25
bent-over barbell rows	3	25
leg curls	3	25
standing calf raises	3	25
cable crossovers	2	25

Day 3

exercise	sets	reps
barbell bench press	3	25
seated cable rows	3	25
squats	3	25
dumbbell military press	3	25
lunges	3	25
front raises	2	25

Program Level II
Endurance/Fat Burning Training
Three-Day Split four days a week
Antagonistic Training

Weeks 1 and 2

Day 1

exercise	sets	reps
barbell bench press	3	20
dumbbell incline bench press	2	20
seated cable rows	3	20
bent-over barbell rows	2	20

Day 2

exercise	sets	reps
triceps kickbacks	2	20
bench dips	2	20
dumbbell curls	2	20
incline curls	2	20

Day 3

exercise	sets	reps
squats	3	20
leg curls	2	20
dumbbell military press	3	20
upright rows	3	20

Weeks 3 and 4

Day 1

exercise	sets	reps
dumbbell bench press	3	25
incline barbell bench press	2	25
one-arm dumbbell rows	3	25
T-bar rows	2	25

Day 2

exercise	sets	reps
preacher curls	2	25
reverse curls	2	25
barbell triceps curls	2	25
bench dips	2	25

Day 3

exercise	sets	reps
leg press	3	25
lunges	3	25
barbell military press	3	25
front raises	2	25

Program Level II
Endurance/Fat Burning Training
Three-Day Split four days a week
Synergistic Training

Weeks 1 and 2

Day 1

exercise	sets	reps
dumbbell bench press	3	20
incline barbell bench press	3	20
triceps kickbacks	2	20
bench dips	2	failure

Day 2

exercise	sets	reps
seated cable rows	3	20
bent-over barbell rows	3	20
dumbbell curls	2	20
incline curls	2	20

Day 3

exercise	sets	reps
squats	3	20
leg extensions	2	20
dumbbell military press	3	20
upright rows	3	20

Weeks 3 and 4

Day 1

exercise	sets	reps
barbell bench press	3	25
dumbbell incline bench press	3	25
triceps curls	3	25
bench dips	2	failure

Day 2

exercise	sets	reps
one-arm rows	3	25
T- bar rows	3	25
preacher curls	2	25
barbell curls	2	25

Day 3

exercise	sets	reps
leg press	3	25
lunges	3	25
barbell military press	3	25
front raises	2	25

Program Level III
Endurance/Fat Burning Training
Three-Day Split four days a week--Antagonistic Training

Weeks 1 and 2

Day 1

exercise	sets	reps
barbell bench press	3	20
dumbbell incline bench press	2	20
seated cable rows	3	20
bent-over barbell rows	2	20
dips	3	failure
wide-grip lat pull downs	2	20

Day 2

exercise	sets	reps
triceps kickbacks	2	20
bench dips	2	20
dumbbell curls	2	20
incline curls	2	20
hammer curls	2	20
close-grip bench press	2	20

Day 3

exercise	sets	reps
squats	3	20
leg extensions	2	20
dumbbell military press	3	20
upright rows	3	20
lunges	2	20
bent-over lateral raises	2	20

Weeks 3 and 4

Day 1

exercise	sets	reps
dumbbell bench press	3	25
incline barbell bench press	2	25
one-arm dumbbell rows	3	25
T-bar rows	2	25
cable crossovers	2	25
close-grip lat pull downs	2	25

Day 2

exercise	sets	reps
preacher curls	2	25
reverse curls	2	25
dumbbell triceps curls	2	25
bench dips	2	25
triceps pull downs	2	25
barbell curls	2	25

Day 3

exercise	sets	reps
leg press	3	25
lunges	3	25
barbell Military press	3	25
lateral raises	2	25
seated calf raises	3	25
cable lateral raises	2	25

Program Level III
Endurance/Fat Burning Training
Three-Day Split four days a week--Synergistic Training

Weeks 1 and 2

Day 1

exercise	sets	reps
dumbbell bench press	3	20
incline barbell bench press	3	20
triceps kickbacks	2	20
bench dips	2	failure
close-grip bench press	2	20
dips	3	failure

Day 2

exercise	sets	reps
seated cable rows	3	20
bent-over barbell rows	3	20
dumbbell curls	2	20
incline curls	2	20
wide-grip lat pull downs	3	20
hammer curls	3	20

Day 3

exercise	sets	reps
squats	3	20
leg curls	2	20
dumbbell military press	3	20
upright rows	3	20
lunges	2	20
bent-over lateral raises	2	20

Weeks 3 and 4

Day 1

exercise	sets	reps
barbell bench press	3	25
incline dumbbell bench press	3	25
triceps curls	3	25
bench dips	2	failure
cable crossovers	2	25
dips	3	failure

Day 2

exercise	sets	reps
one-arm dumbbell rows	3	25
T- bar rows	3	25
preacher curls	2	25
barbell curls	2	25
close-grip lat pull downs	3	25
concentration curls	2	25

Day 3

exercise	sets	reps
leg press	3	25
lunges	3	25
barbell military press	3	25
lateral raises	2	25
seated calf raises	3	25
cable lateral raises	2	25

Program Level III
Endurance/Fat Burning Training

Two-Day Split 4 days per week
Upper & lower body training on the same day
Antagonistic Training

Weeks 1 and 2

Days 1 and 3

exercise	sets	reps
barbell bench press	3	20
dumbbell military press	3	20
wide-grip pull-ups	3	20
leg press	3	20

Days 2 and 4

exercise	sets	reps
leg curls	3	20
standing calf raises	3	20
dumbbell curls	2	20
triceps curls	2	20

Weeks 3 and 4

Days 1 and 3

exercise	sets	reps
dumbbell bench press	3	25
barbell military press	3	25
close-grip lat pull downs	3	25
leg curls	2	25

Days 2 and 4

exercise	sets	reps
squats	3	25
seated calf raises	2	25
barbell curls	2	25
one-arm triceps extension	2	25

Program Level III
Endurance/Fat Burning Training

Two-Day Split 4 days per week
Upper & lower body training on different days

Weeks 1 and 2

Days 1 and 3

exercise	sets	reps
barbell bench press	3	20,20,20
barbell military press	3	20,20,20
bent-over dumbbell rows	3	20,20,20
hammer curls	2	20,20

Days 2 and 4

exercise	sets	reps
squats	3	20,20,20
leg press	3	20,20,20
seated calf raises	3	20,20,20
lunges	2	20,20

Weeks 3 and 4

Days 1 and 3

exercise	sets	reps
dumbbell bench press	3	25,25,25
dumbbell military press	3	25,25,25
bent-over barbell rows	3	25,25,25
reverse dumbbell curls	2	25,25

Days 2 and 4

exercise	sets	reps
leg press	3	20,20,20
lunges	2	20,20,20
squats	3	20,20,20
standing calf raises	3	20,20

Program Level III
Endurance/Fat Burning Training

Two-Day Split 4 days per week

Upper & lower body training on the same day -- Synergistic Training

Weeks 1 and 2

Days 1 and 3

exercise	sets	reps
barbell bench press	3	20
dumbbell incline bench press	2	20
standing flyes	3	20
leg press	3	20

Days 2 and 4

exercise	sets	reps
wide-grip pull-ups	2	failure
hammer curls	2	20
leg curls	3	20
standing calf raises	3	20

Weeks 3 and 4

Days 1 and 3

exercise	sets	reps
dumbbell bench press	3	25
barbell incline bench press	2	25
upright rows	3	25
squats	3	25

Days 2 and 4

exercise	sets	reps
close-grip pull-ups	2	failure
reverse curls	2	25
leg curls	3	25
seated calf raises	2	25

Program Level III
Endurance/Fat Burning Training

Entire body every training day -- Rest every other day

Weeks 1 and 2

Day 1

exercise	sets	reps
barbell bench press	3	20
seated cable rows	3	20
squats	3	20
dumbbell military press	3	20
lunges	3	20
front raises	2	20
incline flyes	2	20
wide-grip pull-ups	2	failure

Day 2

exercise	sets	reps
dumbbell bench press	3	20
standing flyes	3	20
bent-over barbell rows	3	20
leg curls	3	20
standing calf raises	3	20
cable crossovers	2	20
barbell military press	2	20
close-grip pull ups	2	failure

Day 3

exercise	sets	reps
bench	3	20
seated cable rows	3	20
squats	3	20
dumbbell military	3	20
lunges	3	20
front raises	2	20
incline flys	2	20
wide-grip pull ups	2	failure

Weeks 3 and 4

Day 1

exercise	sets	reps
barbell bench press	3	25
seated cable rows	3	25
squats	3	25
dumbbell military press	3	25
lunges	3	25
front raises	2	25
incline flyes	2	25
wide-grip pull-ups	2	failure

Day 2

exercise	sets	reps
dumbbell bench press	3	25
standing flyes	3	25
bent-over barbell rows	3	25
leg curls	3	25
standing calf raises	3	25
cable crossovers	2	25
barbell military press	2	25
close-grip pull-ups	2	failure

Day 3

exercise	sets	reps
barbell bench press	3	25
seated cable rows	3	25
squats	3	25
dumbbell military press	3	25
lunges	3	25
front raises	2	25
incline flyes	2	25
wide-grip pull-ups	2	failure

Program Level IV
Endurance/Fat Burning Training

Three-Day Split four days a week -- Antagonistic Training

Weeks 1 and 2

Day 1

exercise	sets	reps
barbell bench press	3	20
dumbbell incline bench press	2	20
seated cable rows	3	20
bent-over barbell rows	2	20
dips	3	failure
wide-grip lat pull downs	2	20
flyes	2	20
wide-grip pull-ups	2	failure

Day 2

exercise	sets	reps
triceps kickbacks	2	20
bench dips	2	20
dumbbell curls	2	20
incline curls	2	20
hammer curls	2	20
close-grip bench press	2	20
triceps push downs	2	20
behind back wrist curls	2	20

Day 3

exercise	sets	reps
squats	3	20
leg curls	2	20
dumbbell military press	3	20
upright rows	3	20
lunges	2	20
bent-over lateral raises	2	20
standing flyes	2	20
standing calf raises	3	20

Weeks 3 and 4

Day 1

exercise	sets	reps
dumbbell bench press	3	25
incline barbell bench press	2	25
one-arm dumbbell rows	3	25
T-bar rows	2	25
cable crossovers	2	25
close-grip lat pull downs	2	25
dips	3	failure
close-grip pull-ups	2	failure

Day 2

exercise	sets	reps
preacher curls	2	25
reverse curls	2	25
barbell triceps curls	2	25
bench dips	2	25
triceps pull downs	2	25
barbell curls	2	25
reverse wrist curls	2	25
one-arm triceps extensions	2	25

Day 3

exercise	sets	reps
leg press	3	25
lunges	3	25
barbell military press	3	25
lateral raises	2	25
seated calf raises	3	25
cable lateral raises	2	25
dumbbell shrugs	3	25
leg curls	2	25

Program Level IV
Endurance/Fat Burning Training
Three-Day Split four days a week -- Synergistic Training

Weeks 1 and 2

Day 1

exercise	sets	reps
barbell bench press	3	10,10,10
dumbbell incline bench press	3	12,12,12
bench dips	3	failure
dumbbells triceps curls	3	15,15,15
cable crossovers	3	15,15,15
one-arm triceps extensions	3	15,15,15
dips	3	failure
triceps kickbacks	3	15,15,15

Day 2

exercise	sets	reps
wide-grip lat pull down	3	10,10,10
T-bar row	3	12,12,12
barbell curls	3	failure
concentration curls	3	15,15,15
seated cable rows	3	15,15,15
bent-over barbell rows	3	15,15,15
hammer curls	3	12,12,12
preacher curls	3	15,15,15

Day 3

exercise	sets	reps
jump squats	3	10,10,10
power cleans	3	12,12,12
dumbbell military press	3	10,10,10
push press	3	12,12,12
leg press	3	8,8,8
bent-over lateral raises	3	15,15,15
standing flyes	3	12,12,12
standing calf raises	3	20,20,20

Weeks 3 and 4

Day 1

exercise	sets	reps
dumbbell bench press	3	10,10,10
incline barbell bench press	3	12,12,12
close-grip bench press	3	12,12,12
skull crushers	3	15,15,15
incline flyes	3	15,15,15
triceps push downs	3	15,15,15
dips	3	failure
one-arm triceps extensions	3	15,15,15

Day 2

exercise	sets	reps
close-grip pull-ups	3	failure
seated cable rows	3	10,10,10
preacher curls	3	15,15,15
concentration curls	3	15,15,15
bent-over dumbbell rows	3	12,12,12
hammer curls	3	15,15,15
reverse wrist curls	3	15,15,15
close-grip lat pull downs	3	12,12,12

Day 3

exercise	sets	reps
jump squats	3	10,10,10
box steps	3	12,12,12
barbell military press	3	10,10,10
push press	3	12,12,12
squats	3	8,8,8
upright rows	3	12,12,12
front raises	3	15,15,15
seated calf raises	3	20,20,20

Program Level IV
Endurance/Fat Burning Training

Two-Day Split 4 days per week
Upper & lower body training on the same day
Antagonistic Training

Weeks 1 and 2

Days 1 and 3

exercise	sets	reps
barbell bench press	3	10,10,10
wide-grip pull-ups	2	failure
push press	3	12,12,12
leg curls	3	12,12,12
standing calf raises	3	20,20,20
dips	2	failure

Days 2 and 4

exercise	sets	reps
leg press	3	12,12,12
power cleans	3	12,12,12
bench dips	2	failure
preacher curls	4	12,12,12,12
reverse curls	3	12,12,12
triceps kickbacks	4	12,12,12

Weeks 3 and 4

Days 1 and 3

exercise	sets	reps
dumbbell bench press	3	12,12,12
close-grip pull-ups	3	failure
push press	3	12,12,12
leg curls	3	15,15,15
standing calf raises	3	20,20,20
dips	3	failure

Days 2 and 4

exercise	sets	reps
power cleans	3	10,10,10
box steps	3	12,12,12
concentration curls	4	15,15,15,15
triceps curls	4	15,15,15,15
bench dips	3	failure
hammer curls	3	12,12,12

Program Level IV
Endurance/Fat Burning Training

Two-Day Split 4 days per week
Upper & lower body training on different days

Weeks 1 and 2

Days 1 and 3

exercise	sets	reps
barbell bench press	3	10,10,10
push press	3	12,12,12
wide-grip pull-ups	2	failure
reverse curls	3	15,15,15
dips	2	failure
bent-over dumbbell rows	3	12,12,12

Days 2 and 4

exercise	sets	reps
jump squats	3	10,10,10
power cleans	3	12,12,12
squats	3	8,8,8
lunges	3	10,10,10
box steps	3	12,12,12
standing calf raises	3	20,20,20

Weeks 3 and 4

Days 1 and 3

exercise	sets	reps
dumbbell bench press	3	10,10,10
push press	3	12,12,12
close-grip pull-ups	3	failure
hammer curls	3	15,15,15
cable crossovers	3	10,10,10
T-bar rows	3	12,12,12

Days 2 and 4

exercise	sets	reps
squats	3	8,8,8
lunges	3	10,10,10
jump squats	3	10,10,10
power cleans	3	12,12,12
box steps	3	12,12,12
standing calf raises	3	20,20,20

Program Level IV
Endurance/Fat Burning Training

Two-Day Split 4 days per week

Upper & lower body training on the same day -- Synergistic Training

Weeks 1 and 2

Days 1 and 3

exercise	sets	reps
barbell bench press	3	20
dumbbell incline bench press	2	20
standing flyes	3	20
leg press	3	20
dips	2	failure
lunges	2	20

Days 2 and 4

exercise	sets	reps
wide-grip pull-ups	2	failure
hammer curls	2	20
leg curls	3	20
standing calf raises	3	20
seated rows	3	20
dumbbell curls	2	20

Weeks 3 and 4

Days 1 and 3

exercise	sets	reps
dumbbell bench press	3	25
incline barbell bench press	2	25
upright rows	3	25
squats	3	25
leg extensions	2	25
bench dips	3	failure

Days 2 and 4

exercise	sets	reps
close-grip pull-ups	2	failure
reverse curls	2	25
leg curls	3	25
seated calf raises	2	25
one-arm dumbbell rows	3	25
incline dumbbell curls	2	25

Program Level V
Endurance/Fat Burning Training

Two-Day Split 4 days per week

Upper & lower body training on the same day -- Antagonistic Training

Weeks 1 and 2

Days 1 and 3

exercise	sets	reps
barbell bench press	3	20
dumbbell military press	3	20
wide-grip pull ups	3	20
leg press	3	20
incline flyes	2	20
lunges	2	20
seated rows	2	20
dips	2	failure

Days 2 and 4

exercise	sets	reps
leg curls	3	20
standing calf raises	3	20
dumbbell curls	2	20
triceps curls	2	20
hammer curls	2	20
triceps kickbacks	2	20
seated calf raises	2	20
bench dips	2	failure

Weeks 3 and 4

Days 1 and 3

exercise	sets	reps
dumbbell bench press	3	25
barbell military press	3	25
close-grip pull downs	3	25
leg curls	2	25
incline barbell bench press	2	25
leg extensions	2	25
dips	3	failure
close-grip pull-ups	2	failure

Days 2 and 4

exercise	sets	reps
squats	3	25
seated calf raises	2	25
barbell curls	2	25
one-arm triceps extension	2	25
reverse curls	2	25
bench dips	3	failure
standing calf raises	3	25
skull crushers	2	25

Program Level V
Endurance/Fat Burning Training

Two-Day Split 4 days per week
Upper & lower body training on different days

Weeks 1 and 2

Days 1 and 3

exercise	sets	reps
barbell bench press	3	20,20,20
barbell Military press	3	20,20,20
bent-over dumbbell rows	3	20,20,20
hammer curls	2	20,20
dips	2	failure
wide-grip pull ups	2	failure
cable crossovers	2	20,20
skull crushers	2	20,20

Days 2 and 4

exercise	sets	reps
squats	3	20,20,20
leg press	3	20,20,20
standing calf raises	3	20,20,20
lunges	2	20,20
leg extensions	2	20,20
leg curls	2	20,20
seated calf raises	2	20,20
dead lift	2	20,20

Weeks 3 and 4

Days 1 and 3

exercise	sets	reps
dumbbell bench press	3	25,25,25
dumbbell military press	3	25,25,25
bent-over barbell rows	3	25,25,25
reverse curls	2	25,25
close-grip pull ups	3	failure
dumbbell curls	2	25,25
incline flyes	2	25,25
dips	3	25,25,25

Days 2 and 4

exercise	sets	reps
squats	3	25,25,25
leg extensions	2	25,25
leg curls	2	25,25
leg press	3	25,25,25
dead lift	2	25,25
lunges	2	25,25
standing calf raises	3	25,25,25
seated calf raises	2	25,25

Program Level V

Endurance/Fat Burning Training

Two-Day Split 4 days per week
Upper & lower body training on the same day
Synergistic Training

Weeks 1 and 2

Days 1 and 3

exercise	sets	reps
barbell bench press	3	20
dumbbell incline bench press	2	20
standing flyes	3	20
leg press	3	20
dips	2	failure
lunges	2	20
bench dips	2	failure
dumbbell military press	3	20

Days 2 and 4

exercise	sets	reps
wide-grip pull-ups	2	failure
hammer curls	2	20
leg curls	3	20
standing calf raises	3	20
seated rows	3	20
dumbbell curls	2	20
seated calf raises	2	20
wide-grip pull downs	2	20

Weeks 3 and 4

Days 1 and 3

exercise	sets	reps
dumbbell bench press	3	25
Incline barbell bench press	2	25
upright rows	3	25
squats	3	25
leg extensions	2	25
bench dips	3	failure
dips	3	failure
front raises	2	25

Days 2 and 4

exercise	sets	reps
close-grip pull-ups	2	failure
reverse curls	2	25
leg curls	3	25
seated calf raises	2	25
one-arm dumbbell rows	3	25
incline dumbbell curls	2	25
standing calf raises	3	25
close-grip pull downs	2	25

Power/ General Fitness Training

Program Level I
Power/General Fitness Training

Entire body every training day
Rest every other day

Weeks 1 and 2

Day 1

exercise	sets	reps
barbell bench press	3	12,12,12
push press	3	10,10,10
wide-grip pull-ups	2	failure
power cleans	3	12,12,12

Day 2

exercise	sets	reps
dumbbell incline bench press	3	12,12,12
upright rows	3	10,10,10
close-grip pull-ups	2	failure
leg curls	3	12,12,12

Day 3

exercise	sets	reps
dumbbell bench press	3	12,12,12
push press	3	10,10,10
wide-grip pull-ups	2	failure
power cleans	3	12,12,12

Weeks 3 and 4

Day 1

exercise	sets	reps
barbell bench press	3	12,12,12
push press	3	10,10,10
wide-grip pull-ups	2	failure
power cleans	3	12,12,12

Day 2

exercise	sets	reps
dumbbell incline bench press	3	12,12,12
upright rows	3	10,10,10
close-grip pull-ups	2	failure
leg curls	3	12,12,12

Day 3

exercise	sets	reps
dumbbell bench press	3	12,12,12
push press	3	10,10,10
wide-grip pull-ups	2	failure
power cleans	3	12,12,12

Program Level II
Power/General Fitness Training

Entire body every training day
Rest every other day

Weeks 1 and 2

Day 1

exercise	sets	reps
barbell bench press	3	12,12,12
push press	3	10,10,10
wide-grip pull-ups	2	failure
power cleans	3	12,12,12
jump squats	3	10,10,10
standing flyes	3	15,15,15

Day 2

exercise	sets	reps
dumbbell incline bench press	3	12,12,12
upright rows	3	10,10,10
close-grip pull-ups	2	failure
leg curls	3	12,12,12
barbell military press	3	10,10,10
standing calf raises	3	20,20,20

Day 3

exercise	sets	reps
dumbbell bench press	3	12,12,12
push press	3	10,10,10
wide-grip pull-ups	2	failure
power cleans	3	12,12,12
box steps	3	10,10,10
standing flyes	3	15,15,15

Weeks 3 and 4

Day 1

exercise	sets	reps
barbell bench press	3	12,12,12
push press	3	10,10,10
wide-grip pull-ups	2	failure
power cleans	3	12,12,12
jump squats	3	10,10,10
standing flyes	3	15,15,15

Day 2

exercise	sets	reps
dumbbell incline bench press	3	12,12,12
upright rows	3	10,10,10
close-grip pull-ups	2	failure
leg curls	3	12,12,12
barbell military press	3	10,10,10
standing calf raises	3	20,20,20

Day 3

exercise	sets	reps
dumbbell bench press	3	12,12,12
push press	3	10,10,10
wide-grip pull-ups	2	failure
power cleans	3	12,12,12
box steps	3	10,10,10
standing flyes	3	15,15,15

Program Level II
Power/General Fitness Training
Three-Day Split four days a week
Antagonistic Training

Weeks 1 and 2

Day 1

exercise	sets	reps
barbell bench press	3	10,10,10
incline dumbbell bench press	3	12,12,12
wide-grip pull-ups	3	failure
T-bar rows	3	10,10,10

Day 2

exercise	sets	reps
bench dips	3	failure
dumbbell triceps curls	3	15,15,15
barbell curls	3	15,15,15
Incline dumbbell curls	3	15,15,15

Day 3

exercise	sets	reps
jump squats	3	10,10,10
power cleans	3	12,12,12
dumbbell military press	3	10,10,10
push press	3	12,12,12

Weeks 3 and 4

Day 1

exercise	sets	reps
dumbbell bench press	3	10,10,10
incline barbell bench press	3	12,12,12
close-grip pull-ups	3	failure
seated cable rows	3	10,10,10

Day 2

exercise	sets	reps
close-grip bench press	3	15,15,15
skull crushers	3	15,15,15
preacher curls	3	15,15,15
concentration curls	3	15,15,15

Day 3

exercise	sets	reps
jump squats	3	10,10,10
box steps	3	12,12,12
barbell military press	3	10,10,10
push press	3	12,12,12

Program Level II
Power/General Fitness Training
Three-Day Split four days a week
Synergistic Training

Weeks 1 and 2

Day 1

exercise	sets	reps
barbell bench press	3	10,10,10
incline dumbbell bench press	3	12,12,12
bench dips	3	failure
triceps curls	3	15,15,15

Day 2

exercise	sets	reps
wide-grip pull-ups	3	failure
T-bar rows	3	10,10,10
barbell curls	3	15,15,15
incline dumbbell curls	3	15,15,15

Day 3

exercise	sets	reps
jump squats	3	10,10,10
power cleans	3	12,12,12
dumbbell military press	3	10,10,10
push press	3	12,12,12

Weeks 3 and 4

Day 1

exercise	sets	reps
dumbbell bench press	3	10,10,10
incline barbell bench press	3	12,12,12
close-grip bench press	3	12,12,12
skull crushers	3	15,15,15

Day 2

exercise	sets	reps
close-grip pull-ups	3	failure
seated cable rows	3	10,10,10
preacher curls	3	15,15,15
concentration curls	3	15,15,15

Day 3

exercise	sets	reps
jump squats	3	10,10,10
box steps	3	12,12,12
barbell military press	3	10,10,10
push press	3	12,12,12

Program Level III
Power/General Fitness Training
Three-Day Split four days a week
Antagonistic Training

Weeks 1 and 2

Day 1

exercise	sets	reps
barbell bench press	3	10,10,10
dumbbell incline bench press	3	12,12,12
wide-grip pull-ups	3	failure
T-bar rows	3	10,10,10
cable crossovers	3	15,15,15
one-arm dumbbell rows	3	12,12,12

Day 2

exercise	sets	reps
bench dips	3	failure
barbell triceps curls	3	15,15,15
barbell curls	3	15,15,15
incline dumbbell curls	3	15,15,15
reverse curls	3	15,15,15
one-arm triceps extensions	3	15,15,15

Day 3

exercise	sets	reps
jump squats	3	10,10,10
power cleans	3	12,12,12
dumbbell military press	3	10,10,10
push press	3	12,12,12
leg press	3	8,8,8
bent-over lateral raises	3	15,15,15

Weeks 3 and 4

Day 1

exercise	sets	reps
dumbbell bench press	3	10,10,10
incline barbell bench press	3	12,12,12
close-grip pull-ups	3	failure
seated cable rows	3	10,10,10
flyes	3	15,15,15
bent-over barbell rows	3	12,12,12

Day 2

exercise	sets	reps
close-grip bench press	3	15,15,15
skull crushers	3	15,15,15
preacher curls	3	15,15,15
concentration curls	3	15,15,15
hammer curls	3	15,15,15
triceps push downs	3	15,15,15

Day 3

exercise	sets	reps
jump squats	3	10,10,10
box steps	3	12,12,12
barbell military press	3	10,10,10
push press	3	12,12,12
squats	3	8,8,8
upright rows	3	12,12,12

Program Level III
Power/General Fitness Training
Three-Day Split four days a week
Synergistic Training

Weeks 1 and 2

Day 1

exercise	sets	reps
barbell bench press	3	10,10,10
incline dumbbell bench press	3	12,12,12
bench dips	3	failure
dumbbell triceps curls	3	15,15,15
cable crossovers	3	15,15,15
one-arm triceps extensions	3	15,15,15

Day 2

exercise	sets	reps
wide-grip pull-ups	3	failure
T-bar rows	3	10,10,10
barbell curls	3	15,15,15
incline dumbbell curls	3	15,15,15
one-arm dumbbell rows	3	12,12,12
reverse curls	3	15,15,15

Day 3

exercise	sets	reps
jump squats	3	10,10,10
power cleans	3	12,12,12
dumbbell military press	3	10,10,10
push press	3	12,12,12
leg press	3	8,8,8
bent-over lateral raises	3	15,15,15

Weeks 3 and 4

Day 1

exercise	sets	reps
dumbbell bench press	3	10,10,10
incline barbell bench press	3	12,12,12
close-grip bench press	3	12,12,12
skull crushers	3	15,15,15
incline flyes	3	15,15,15
triceps push downs	3	15,15,15

Day 2

exercise	sets	reps
close-grip pull-ups	3	failure
seated cable rows	3	10,10,10
preacher curls	3	15,15,15
concentration curls	3	15,15,15
bent-over dumbbell rows	3	12,12,12
hammer curls	3	15,15,15

Day 3

exercise	sets	reps
jump squats	3	10,10,10
box steps	3	12,12,12
barbell military press	3	10,10,10
push press	3	12,12,12
squats	3	8,8,8
upright rows	3	12,12,12

Program Level III
Power/General Fitness Training

Two-Day Split 4 days per week

Upper & lower body training on the same day -- Antagonistic Training

Weeks 1 and 2

Days 1 and 3

exercise	sets	reps
squats	5	10,8,6,4,2
dead lift	5	10,8,6,4,2
preacher curls	4	12,10,8,6
triceps push downs	4	12,10,8,6

Days 2 and 4

exercise	sets	reps
calf raises	3	20,20,20
power cleans	3	12,12,12
bench dips	2	failure
preacher curls	4	12,12,12,12

Weeks 3 and 4

Days 1 and 3

exercise	sets	reps
dumbbell bench press	3	12,12,12
close-grip pull-ups	3	failure
push press	3	12,12,12
leg curls	3	15,15,15

Days 2 and 4

exercise	sets	reps
power cleans	3	10,10,10
box steps	3	12,12,12
concentration curls	4	15,15,15,15
triceps curls	4	15,15,15,15

Program Level III
Power/General Fitness Training

Two-Day Split 4 days per week

Upper & lower body training on different days

Weeks 1 and 2

Days 1 and 3

exercise	sets	reps
barbell bench press	3	10,10,10
push press	3	12,12,12
wide-grip pull-ups	2	failure
reverse curls	3	15,15,15

Days 2 and 4

exercise	sets	reps
jump squats	3	10,10,10
cleans	3	12,12,12
lunges	3	10,10,10
standing calf raises	3	20,20,20

Weeks 3 and 4

Days 1 and 3

exercise	sets	reps
dumbbell bench press	3	10,10,10
push press	3	12,12,12
close-grip pull-ups	3	failure
hammer curls	3	15,15,15

Days 2 and 4

exercise	sets	reps
lunges	3	10,10,10
jump squats	3	10,10,10
power cleans	3	12,12,12
standing calf raises	3	20,20,20

Program Level III
Power/General Fitness Training

Two-Day Split 4 days per week

Upper & lower body training on the same day -- Synergistic Training

Weeks 1 and 2

Days 1 and 3

exercise	sets	reps
dumbbell bench press	3	10,10,10
push press	3	12,12,12
dumbbell incline bench press	3	12,12,12
leg curls	3	12,12,12

Days 2 and 4

exercise	sets	reps
wide-grip pull-ups	2	failure
reverse curls	3	12,12,12
squats	4	10,10,10
box steps	3	12,12,12

Weeks 3 and 4

Days 1 and 3

exercise	sets	reps
barbell bench press	3	12,12,12
push press	3	12,12,12
incline barbell bench press	3	12,12,12
standing calf raises	3	20,20,20

Days 2 and 4

exercise	sets	reps
close-grip pull-ups	3	failure
hammer curls	4	12,12,12,12
jump squats	3	10,10,10
power cleans	3	12,12,12

Program Level III
Power/General Fitness Training

Entire body every training day -- Rest every other day

Weeks 1 and 2

Day 1

exercise	sets	reps
barbell bench press	3	12,12,12
push press	3	10,10,10
wide-grip pull-ups	2	failure
power cleans	3	12,12,12
jump squats	3	10,10,10
standing flyes	3	15,15,15
T-bar rows	3	12,12,12
cable crossovers	3	10,10,10

Day 2

exercise	sets	reps
dumbbell incline bench press	3	12,12,12
upright rows	3	10,10,10
close-grip pull-ups	2	failure
leg curls	3	12,12,12
barbell military press	3	10,10,10
standing calf raises	3	20,20,20
seated cable rows	3	12,12,12
incline flyes	3	10,10,10

Day 3

exercise	sets	reps
dumbbell bench press	3	12,12,12
push press	3	10,10,10
wide-grip pull-ups	2	failure
power cleans	3	12,12,12
box steps	3	10,10,10
standing flyes	3	15,15,15
T-bar rows	3	12,12,12
cable crossovers	3	10,10,10

Weeks 3 and 4

Day 1

exercise	sets	reps
barbell bench press	3	12,12,12
push press	3	10,10,10
wide-grip pull-ups	2	failure
power cleans	3	12,12,12
jump squats	3	10,10,10
standing flyes	3	15,15,15
T-bar rows	3	12,12,12
cable crossovers	3	10,10,10

Day 2

exercise	sets	reps
dumbbell incline bench press	3	12,12,12
upright rows	3	10,10,10
close-grip pull-ups	2	failure
leg curls	3	12,12,12
barbell military press	3	10,10,10
standing calf raises	3	20,20,20
seated cable rows	3	12,12,12
incline flyes	3	10,10,10

Day 3

exercise	sets	reps
dumbbell bench press	3	12,12,12
push press	3	10,10,10
wide-grip pull-ups	2	failure
power cleans	3	12,12,12
box steps	3	10,10,10
standing flyes	3	15,15,15
T-bar rows	3	12,12,12
cable crossovers	3	10,10,10

Program Level IV

Power/General Fitness Training

Three-Day Split four days a week -- Antagonistic Training

Weeks 1 and 2

Day 1

exercise	sets	reps
barbell bench press	3	10,10,10
incline dumbbell bench press	3	12,12,12
wide-grip pull-ups	3	failure
T-bar rows	3	10,10,10
cable crossovers	3	15,15,15
one-arm dumbbell rows	3	12,12,12
dips	3	failure
behind the neck pull downs	3	12,12,12

Day 2

exercise	sets	reps
bench dips	3	failure
dumbbell triceps curls	3	15,15,15
barbell curls	3	15,15,15
incline dumbbell curls	3	15,15,15
reverse curls	3	15,15,15
one-arm triceps extensions	3	15,15,15
behind back wrist curls	3	15,15,15
triceps kickbacks	3	15,15,15

Day 3

exercise	sets	reps
jump squats	3	10,10,10
power cleans	3	12,12,12
dumbbell military press	3	10,10,10
push press	3	12,12,12
leg press	3	8,8,8
bent-over lateral raises	3	15,15,15
standing flyes	3	12,12,12
standing calf raises	3	20,20,20

Weeks 3 and 4

Day 1

exercise	sets	reps
jump squats	3	10,10,10
power cleans	3	12,12,12
dumbbell military press	3	10,10,10
push press	3	12,12,12
leg press	3	8,8,8
bent-over lateral raises	3	15,15,15
standing flyes	3	12,12,12
standing calf raises	3	20,20,20

Day 2

exercise	sets	reps
close-grip bench press	3	15,15,15
skull crushers	3	15,15,15
preacher curls	3	15,15,15
concentration curls	3	15,15,15
hammer curls	3	15,15,15
triceps push downs	3	15,15,15
reverse wrist curls	3	15,15,15
barbell triceps curls	3	15,15,15

Day 3

exercise	sets	reps
jump squats	3	10,10,10
box steps	3	12,12,12
barbell military press	3	10,10,10
push press	3	12,12,12
squats	3	8,8,8
upright rows	3	12,12,12
front raises	3	15,15,15
seated calf raises	3	20,20,20

Program Level IV
Power/General Fitness Training
Three-Day Split four days a week -- Synergistic Training

Weeks 1 and 2

Day 1

exercise	sets	reps
barbell bench press	3	10,10,10
dumbbell incline bench press	3	12,12,12
bench dips	3	failure
dumbbells triceps curls	3	15,15,15
cable crossovers	3	15,15,15
one-arm triceps extensions	3	15,15,15
dips	3	failure
triceps kickbacks	3	15,15,15

Day 2

exercise	sets	reps
wide-grip lat pull down	3	10,10,10
T-bar row	3	12,12,12
barbell curls	3	failure
concentration curls	3	15,15,15
seated cable rows	3	15,15,15
bent-over barbell rows	3	15,15,15
hammer curls	3	12,12,12
preacher curls	3	15,15,15

Day 3

exercise	sets	reps
jump squats	3	10,10,10
power cleans	3	12,12,12
dumbbell military press	3	10,10,10
push press	3	12,12,12
leg press	3	8,8,8
bent-over lateral raises	3	15,15,15
standing flyes	3	12,12,12
standing calf raises	3	20,20,20

Weeks 3 and 4

Day 1

exercise	sets	reps
dumbbell bench press	3	10,10,10
incline barbell bench press	3	12,12,12
close-grip bench press	3	12,12,12
skull crushers	3	15,15,15
incline flyes	3	15,15,15
triceps push downs	3	15,15,15
dips	3	failure
one-arm triceps extensions	3	15,15,15

Day 2

exercise	sets	reps
close-grip pull-ups	3	failure
seated cable rows	3	10,10,10
preacher curls	3	15,15,15
concentration curls	3	15,15,15
bent-over dumbbell rows	3	12,12,12
hammer curls	3	15,15,15
reverse wrist curls	3	15,15,15
close-grip lat pull downs	3	12,12,12

Day 3

exercise	sets	reps
jump squats	3	10,10,10
box steps	3	12,12,12
barbell military press	3	10,10,10
push press	3	12,12,12
squats	3	8,8,8
upright rows	3	12,12,12
front raises	3	15,15,15
seated calf raises	3	20,20,20

Program Level IV
Power/General Fitness Training

Two-Day Split 4 days per week

Upper & lower body training on the same day -- Antagonistic Training

Weeks 1 and 2

Days 1 and 3

exercise	sets	reps
barbell bench press	3	10,10,10
wide-grip pull-ups	2	failure
push press	3	12,12,12
leg curls	3	12,12,12
standing calf raises	3	20,20,20
dips	2	failure

Days 2 and 4

exercise	sets	reps
leg press	3	12,12,12
power cleans	3	12,12,12
bench dips	2	failure
preacher curls	4	12,12,12,12
reverse curls	3	12,12,12
triceps kickbacks	4	12,12,12

Weeks 3 and 4

Days 1 and 3

exercise	sets	reps
dumbbell bench press	3	12,12,12
close-grip pull-ups	3	failure
push press	3	12,12,12
leg curls	3	15,15,15
standing calf raises	3	20,20,20
dips	3	failure

Days 2 and 4

exercise	sets	reps
power cleans	3	10,10,10
box steps	3	12,12,12
concentration curls	4	15,15,15,15
triceps curls	4	15,15,15,15
bench dips	3	failure
hammer curls	3	12,12,12

Program Level IV
Power/General Fitness Training

Two-Day Split 4 days per week

Upper & lower body training on different days

Weeks 1 and 2

Days 1 and 3

exercise	sets	reps
barbell bench press	3	10,10,10
push press	3	12,12,12
wide-grip pull-ups	2	failure
reverse curls	3	15,15,15
dips	2	failure
bent-over dumbbell rows	3	12,12,12

Days 2 and 4

exercise	sets	reps
jump squats	3	10,10,10
power cleans	3	12,12,12
squats	3	8,8,8
lunges	3	10,10,10
box steps	3	12,12,12
standing calf raises	3	20,20,20

Weeks 3 and 4

Days 1 and 3

exercise	sets	reps
dumbbell bench press	3	10,10,10
push press	3	12,12,12
close-grip pull-ups	3	failure
hammer curls	3	15,15,15
cable crossovers	3	10,10,10
T-bar rows	3	12,12,12

Days 2 and 4

exercise	sets	reps
squats	3	8,8,8
lunges	3	10,10,10
jump squats	3	10,10,10
power cleans	3	12,12,12
box steps	3	12,12,12
standing calf raises	3	20,20,20

Program Level IV
Power/General Fitness Training

Two-Day Split 4 days per week
Upper & lower body training on the same day -- Synergistic Training

Weeks 1 and 2

Days 1 and 3

exercise	sets	reps
dumbbell bench press	3	10,10,10
push press	3	12,12,12
dumbbell incline bench press	3	12,12,12
leg curls	3	12,12,12
dips	2	failure
standing calf raises	3	20,20,20

Days 2 and 4

exercise	sets	reps
wide-grip pull-ups	2	failure
reverse curls	3	12,12,12
squats	4	10,10,10
box steps	3	12,12,12
T-bar rows	3	12,12,12
power cleans	3	10,10,10

Weeks 3 and 4

Days 1 and 3

exercise	sets	reps
barbell bench press	3	12,12,12
push press	3	12,12,12
incline barbell bench press	3	12,12,12
standing calf raises	3	20,20,20
leg curls	4	10,10,10
bench dips	3	failure

Days 2 and 4

exercise	sets	reps
close-grip pull-ups	3	failure
hammer curls	4	12,12,12,12
jump squats	3	10,10,10
power cleans	3	12,12,12
box steps	3	12,12,12
one-arm dumbbell rows	3	12,12,12

Program Level V
Power/General Fitness Training

Two-Day Split 4 days per week
Upper & lower body training on the same day -- Antagonistic Training

Weeks 1 and 2

Days 1 and 3

exercise	sets	reps
barbell bench press	3	10,10,10
wide-grip pull-ups	2	failure
push press	3	12,12,12
leg curls	3	12,12,12
standing calf raises	3	20,20,20
dips	2	failure
one-arm dumbbell rows	3	12,12,12
barbell military press	3	10,10,10

Days 2 and 4

exercise	sets	reps
leg press	3	12,12,12
power cleans	3	12,12,12
bench dips	2	failure
preacher curls	4	12,12,12,12
reverse curls	3	12,12,12
triceps kickbacks	4	12,12,12
leg extension	3	15,15,15
close-grip bench press	3	10,10,10

Weeks 3 and 4

Days 1 and 3

exercise	sets	reps
dumbbell bench press	3	12,12,12
close-grip pull-ups	3	failure
push press	3	12,12,12
leg curls	3	15,15,15
standing calf raises	3	20,20,20
dips	3	failure
cable crossovers	3	10,10,10
bent-over lateral raises	3	15,15,15

Days 2 and 4

exercise	sets	reps
power cleans	3	10,10,10
box steps	3	12,12,12
concentration curls	4	15,15,15,15
triceps curls	4	15,15,15,15
bench dips	3	failure
hammer curls	3	12,12,12
jump squats	3	12,12,12
one-arm triceps extensions	3	12,12,12

Program Level V
Power/General Fitness Training

Two-Day Split 4 days per week
Upper & lower body training on different days

Weeks 1 and 2

Days 1 and 3

exercise	sets	reps
barbell bench press	3	10,10,10
push press	3	12,12,12
wide-grip pull-ups	2	failure
reverse curls	3	15,15,15
dips	2	failure
bent-over dumbbell rows	3	12,12,12
incline flyes	3	12,12,12
triceps push downs	3	15,15,15

Days 2 and 4

exercise	sets	reps
jump squats	3	10,10,10
power cleans	3	12,12,12
squats	3	8,8,8
lunges	3	10,10,10
box steps	3	12,12,12
leg curls	3	12,12,12
leg extensions	3	12,12,12
standing calf raises	3	20,20,20

Weeks 3 and 4

Days 1 and 3

exercise	sets	reps
dumbbell bench press	3	10,10,10
push press	3	12,12,12
close-grip pull-ups	3	failure
hammer curls	3	15,15,15
cable crossovers	3	10,10,10
T-bar rows	3	12,12,12
incline bench press	3	12,12,12
bench dips	3	15,15,15

Days 2 and 4

exercise	sets	reps
squats	3	8,8,8
box steps	3	12,12,12
power cleans	3	12,12,12
jump squats	3	10,10,10
lunges	3	10,10,10
leg curls	3	12,12,12
leg extensions	3	12,12,12
standing calf raises	3	20,20,20

Program Level V
Power/General Fitness Training

Two-Day Split 4 days per week
Upper & lower body training on the same day

Weeks 1 and 2

Days 1 and 3

exercise	sets	reps
dumbbell bench press	3	10,10,10
push press	3	12,12,12
dumbbell incline bench press	3	12,12,12
leg curls	3	12,12,12
dips	2	failure
standing calf raises	3	20,20,20
bench dips	2	failure
bent-over lateral raises	3	15,15,15

Days 2 and 4

exercise	sets	reps
dumbbell bench press	3	10,10,10
push press	3	12,12,12
dumbbell incline bench press	3	12,12,12
leg curls	3	12,12,12
dips	2	failure
standing calf raises	3	20,20,20
behind the neck pull downs	3	12,12,12
concentration curls	4	15,15,15,15

Weeks 3 and 4

Days 1 and 3

exercise	sets	reps
barbell bench press	3	12,12,12
push press	3	12,12,12
incline barbell bench press	3	12,12,12
standing calf raises	3	20,20,20
leg curls	4	10,10,10
bench dips	3	failure
dips	3	failure
upright rows	3	12,12,12

Days 2 and 4

exercise	sets	reps
close-grip pull-ups	3	failure
hammer curls	4	12,12,12,12
jump squats	3	10,10,10
power cleans	3	12,12,12
box steps	3	12,12,12
one-arm dumbbell rows	3	12,12,12
T-bar rows	3	10,10,10
dumbbell curls	3	12,12,12

Strength Training

Program Level I

Strength Training

Entire body every training day
Rest every other day

Weeks 1 and 2

Day 1

exercise	sets	reps
barbell bench press	5	8,6,4,2,1
barbell military press	5	8,6,4,2,1
wide-grip lat pull downs	4	8,8,8,8
squats	5	10,8,6,4,2

Day 2

exercise	sets	reps
incline barbell bench press	5	8,6,4,2,1
barbell military press	5	8,6,4,2,1
close-grip lat pull downs	4	8,8,8,8
leg press	5	10,8,6,4,2

Day 3

exercise	sets	reps
barbell bench press	5	8,6,4,2,1
barbell military press	5	8,6,4,2,1
wide-grip lat pull downs	4	8,8,8,8
squats	5	10,8,6,4,2

Weeks 3 and 4

Day 1

exercise	sets	reps
barbell bench press	5	8,6,4,2,1
barbell military press	5	8,6,4,2,1
T-bar rows	4	8,8,8,8
leg press	5	10,8,6,4,2

Day 2

exercise	sets	reps
incline barbell bench press	5	8,6,4,2,1
barbell military press	5	8,6,4,2,1
seated cable rows	4	8,8,8,8
squats	5	10,8,6,4,2

Day 3

exercise	sets	reps
barbell bench press	5	8,6,4,2,1
barbell military press	5	8,6,4,2,1
bent-over barbell rows	4	8,8,8,8
leg press	5	10,8,6,4,2

Program Level II

Strength Training

Three-Day Split four days a week
Antagonistic Training

Weeks 1 and 2

Day 1

exercise	sets	reps
barbell bench press	5	8,6,4,2,1
incline barbell bench press	5	8,6,4,2,1
wide-grip lat pull downs	4	8,8,8,8
seated cable rows	4	8,8,8,8

Day 2

exercise	sets	reps
squats	5	10,8,6,4,2
leg press	5	10,8,6,4,2
barbell military press	5	8,6,4,2,1
upright rows	4	8,8,6,6

Day 3

exercise	sets	reps
barbell triceps curls	5	12,10,8,6,2
close-grip barbell bench press	5	12,10,8,6,2
hammer curls	4	12,10,8,6
preacher curls	4	12,10,8,6

Weeks 3 and 4

Day 1

exercise	sets	reps
barbell bench press	5	8,6,4,2,1
incline barbell bench press	5	8,6,4,2,1
close-grip lat pull downs	4	8,8,8,8
T-bar rows	4	8,8,8,8

Day 2

exercise	sets	reps
squats	5	10,8,6,4,2
dead lift	5	10,8,6,4,2
barbell military press	5	8,6,4,2,1
standing flyes	4	8,8,6,6

Day 3

exercise	sets	reps
barbell triceps curls	5	12,10,8,6,2
triceps push downs	5	12,10,8,6,2
reverse barbell curls	4	12,10,8,6
barbell curls	4	12,10,8,6

Program Level II

Strength Training

Three-Day Split four days a week
Synergistic Training

Weeks 1 and 2

Day 1

exercise	sets	reps
barbell bench press	5	8,6,4,2,1
incline barbell bench press	5	8,6,4,2,1
close-grip barbell bench press	5	8,6,4,2,1
triceps push downs	4	12,10,8,6

Day 2

exercise	sets	reps
wide-grip lat pull downs	4	8,8,8,8
hammer curls	4	12,10,8,6
preacher curls	4	12,10,8,6
bent-over barbell rows	4	8,8,8,8

Day 3

exercise	sets	reps
squats	5	10,8,6,4,2
leg press	5	10,8,6,4,2
barbell military press	5	8,6,4,2,1
upright rows	4	8,8,6,6

Weeks 3 and 4

Day 1

exercise	sets	reps
incline barbell bench press	5	8,6,4,2,1
barbell triceps curls	4	12,10,8,6
flyes	4	8,8,6,6
skull crushers	4	12,10,8,6

Day 2

exercise	sets	reps
close-grip lat pull downs	4	8,8,8,8
reverse barbell curls	4	12,10,8,6
T-bar rows	4	8,8,8,8
concentration curls	4	12,10,8,6

Day 3

exercise	sets	reps
squats	5	10,8,6,4,2
barbell military press	5	8,6,4,2,1
standing flyes	4	8,8,6,6
dead lift	5	10,8,6,4,2

Program Level II

Strength Training

Entire body every training day
Rest every other day

Weeks 1 and 2

Day 1

exercise	sets	reps
barbell bench press	5	8,6,4,2,1
barbell military press	5	8,6,4,2,1
wide-grip lat pull downs	4	8,8,8,8
squats	5	10,8,6,4,2
incline barbell bench press	4	8,6,4,2
lunges	4	10,8,8,6

Day 2

exercise	sets	reps
incline barbell bench press	5	8,6,4,2,1
barbell military press	5	8,6,4,2,1
close-grip lat pull downs	4	8,8,8,8
leg press	5	10,8,6,4,2
barbell bench press	4	8,6,4,2
dead lift	5	10,8,6,4,2

Day 3

exercise	sets	reps
barbell bench press	5	8,6,4,2,1
barbell military press	5	8,6,4,2,1
wide-grip lat pull downs	4	8,8,8,8
squats	5	10,8,6,4,2
incline dumbbell bench press	4	8,6,4,2
lunges	4	10,8,8,6

Weeks 3 and 4

Day 1

exercise	sets	reps
barbell bench press	5	8,6,4,2,1
barbell military press	5	8,6,4,2,1
T-bar rows	4	8,8,8,8
leg press	5	10,8,6,4,2
incline barbell bench press	4	8,6,4,2
dead lift	5	10,8,6,4,2

Day 2

exercise	sets	reps
incline barbell bench press	5	8,6,4,2,1
barbell military press	5	8,6,4,2,1
seated cable rows	4	8,8,8,8
squats	5	10,8,6,4,2
incline flyes	4	8,6,4,2
lunges	5	10,8,6,4,2

Day 3

exercise	sets	reps
barbell bench press	5	8,6,4,2,1
barbell military press	5	8,6,4,2,1
bent-over barbell rows	4	8,8,8,8
leg press	5	10,8,6,4,2
incline barbell bench press	4	8,6,4,2
dead lift	5	10,8,6,4,2

Program Level III

Strength Training

Three-Day Split four days a week -- Antagonistic Training

Weeks 1 and 2

Day 1

exercise	sets	reps
barbell bench press	5	8,6,4,2,1
incline barbell bench press	5	8,6,4,2,1
wide-grip lat pull downs	4	8,8,8,8
seated cable rows	4	8,8,8,8
cable crossovers	4	8,8,6,6
bent-over barbell rows	4	8,8,8,8

Day 2

exercise	sets	reps
squats	5	10,8,6,4,2
leg press	5	10,8,6,4,2
barbell military press	5	8,6,4,2,1
upright rows	4	8,8,6,6
lunges	4	10,8,8,6
barbell shrugs	4	10,8,8,6

Day 3

exercise	sets	reps
barbell triceps curls	5	12,10,8,6,2
close-grip barbell bench press	5	12,10,8,6,2
hammer curls	4	12,10,8,6
preacher curls	4	12,10,8,6
bench dips	5	12,10,8,6,2
barbell curls	4	12,10,8,6

Weeks 3 and 4

Day 1

exercise	sets	reps
barbell bench press	5	8,6,4,2,1
incline barbell bench press	5	8,6,4,2,1
close-grip lat pull downs	4	8,8,8,8
T-bar rows	4	8,8,8,8
flyes	4	10,8,8,6
behind the neck pull downs	4	8,8,8,8

Day 2

exercise	sets	reps
squats	5	10,8,6,4,2
dead lift	5	10,8,6,4,2
barbell military press	5	8,6,4,2,1
standing flyes	4	8,8,6,6
lunges	4	10,8,8,6
barbell shrugs	4	10,8,8,6

Day 3

exercise	sets	reps
barbell triceps curls	5	12,10,8,6,2
triceps push downs	5	12,10,8,6,2
reverse barbell curls	4	12,10,8,6
barbell curls	4	12,10,8,6
dips	5	12,10,8,6,2
preacher curls	4	12,10,8,6

Program Level III

Strength Training

Three-Day Split four days a week -- Synergistic Training

Weeks 1 and 2

Day 1

exercise	sets	reps
barbell bench press	5	8,6,4,2,1
incline barbell bench press	5	8,6,4,2,1
close-grip barbell bench press	5	8,6,4,2,1
triceps push downs	4	12,10,8,6
flyes	4	10,8,8,6
skull crushers	5	12,10,8,6,2

Day 2

exercise	sets	reps
wide-grip lat pull downs	4	8,8,8,8
hammer curls	4	12,10,8,6
preacher curls	4	12,10,8,6
bent-over barbell rows	4	8,8,8,8
seated cable rows	4	8,8,8,8
barbell curls	4	12,10,8,6

Day 3

exercise	sets	reps
squats	5	10,8,6,4,2
leg press	5	10,8,6,4,2
barbell military press	5	8,6,4,2,1
upright rows	4	8,8,6,6
lunges	4	10,8,8,6
standing flyes	4	8,8,6,6

Weeks 3 and 4

Day 1

exercise	sets	reps
barbell bench press	5	8,6,4,2,1
incline barbell bench press	5	8,6,4,2,1
triceps kickbacks	5	8,6,4,2,1
triceps pull downs	4	12,10,8,6
incline flyes	4	10,8,8,6
barbell triceps curls	5	12,10,8,6,2

Day 2

exercise	sets	reps
close-grip lat pull downs	4	8,8,8,8
reverse barbell curls	4	12,10,8,6
incline dumbbell curls	4	12,10,8,6
behind the neck pull downs	4	8,8,8,8
T-bar rows	4	8,8,8,8
concentration curls	4	12,10,8,6

Day 3

exercise	sets	reps
squats	5	10,8,6,4,2
dead lift	5	10,8,6,4,2
barbell military press	5	8,6,4,2,1
lateral raises	4	8,8,8,8
leg curls	4	10,8,8,6
upright rows	4	8,8,6,6

Program Level III
Strength Training
Two-Day Split 4 days per week
Upper & lower body training on the same day -- Antagonistic Training

Weeks 1 and 2

Days 1 and 3

exercise	sets	reps
barbell bench press	5	8,6,4,2,1
wide-grip lat pull downs	4	8,8,8,8
barbell military press	5	8,6,4,2,1
leg curls	5	10,8,6,4,2

Days 2 and 4

exercise	sets	reps
squats	5	10,8,6,4,2
leg press	5	10,8,6,4,2
barbell curls	4	12,10,8,6
skull crushers	5	12,10,8,6,2

Weeks 3 and 4

Days 1 and 3

exercise	sets	reps
barbell bench press	5	8,6,4,2,1
close-grip lat pull downs	4	8,8,8,8
barbell military press	5	8,6,4,2,1
leg curls	5	10,8,6,4,2

Days 2 and 4

exercise	sets	reps
squats	5	10,8,6,4,2
dead lift	5	10,8,6,4,2
preacher curls	4	12,10,8,6
triceps push downs	4	12,10,8,6

Program Level III
Strength Training
Two-Day Split 4 days per week
Upper & lower body training on different days

Weeks 1 and 2

Days 1 and 3

exercise	sets	reps
barbell bench press	5	8,6,4,2,1
wide-grip lat pull downs	4	8,8,8,8
barbell military press	5	8,6,4,2,1
hammer curls	4	12,10,8,6

Days 2 and 4

exercise	sets	reps
squats	5	10,8,6,4,2
leg press	5	10,8,6,4,2
lunges	5	10,8,6,4,2
standing calf raises	4	20,20,20,20

Weeks 3 and 4

Days 1 and 3

exercise	sets	reps
barbell bench press	5	8,6,4,2,1
close-grip lat pull downs	4	8,8,8,8
barbell military press	5	8,6,4,2,1
reverse curls	4	12,10,8,6

Days 2 and 4

exercise	sets	reps
leg press	5	10,8,6,4,2
Leg extensions	5	10,8,6,4,2
squats	5	10,8,6,4,2
seated calf raises	4	20,20,20,20

Program Level III
Strength Training

Two-Day Split 4 days per week
Upper & lower body training on the same day -- Synergistic Training

Weeks 1 and 2

Days 1 and 3

exercise	sets	reps
barbell bench press	5	8,6,4,2,1
upright rows	5	8,6,4,2,1
incline barbell bench press	5	8,6,4,2,1
leg curls	5	10,8,6,4,2

Days 2 and 4

exercise	sets	reps
wide-grip lat pull downs	4	8,8,8,8
hammer curls	4	12,10,8,6
squats	5	10,8,6,4,2
leg extensions	4	8,8,6,6

Weeks 3 and 4

Days 1 and 3

exercise	sets	reps
barbell bench press	5	8,6,4,2,1
upright rows	5	8,6,4,2,1
incline barbell bench press	5	8,6,4,2,1
leg curls	5	10,8,6,4,2

Days 2 and 4

exercise	sets	reps
close-grip lat pull downs	4	8,8,8,8
reverse curls	4	12,10,8,6
leg press	5	10,8,6,4,2
leg extensions	4	8,8,6,6

Program Level III
Strength Training

Entire body every training day -- Rest every other day

Weeks 1 and 2

Day 1

exercise	sets	reps
barbell bench press	5	8,6,4,2,1
barbell military press	5	8,6,4,2,1
wide-grip lat pull downs	4	8,8,8,8
squats	5	10,8,6,4,2
incline barbell bench press	4	8,6,4,2
lunges	4	10,8,8,6
bent-over barbell rows	4	8,8,8,8
incline flyes	4	8,8,6,6

Day 2

exercise	sets	reps
incline barbell bench press	5	8,6,4,2,1
barbell military press	5	8,6,4,2,1
close-grip lat pull downs	4	8,8,8,8
leg press	5	10,8,6,4,2
barbell bench press	4	8,6,4,2
dead lift	5	10,8,6,4,2
seated cable rows	4	8,8,8,8
flyes	4	8,8,6,6

Day 3

exercise	sets	reps
barbell bench press	5	8,6,4,2,1
barbell military press	5	8,6,4,2,1
wide-grip lat pull downs	4	8,8,8,8
squats	5	10,8,6,4,2
incline barbell bench press	4	8,6,4,2
lunges	4	10,8,8,6
bent-over barbell rows	4	8,8,8,8
incline flyes	4	8,8,6,6

Weeks 3 and 4

Day 1

exercise	sets	reps
barbell bench press	5	8,6,4,2,1
barbell military press	5	8,6,4,2,1
T-bar rows	4	8,8,8,8
leg press	5	10,8,6,4,2
incline barbell bench press	4	8,6,4,2
dead lift	5	10,8,6,4,2
wide-grip lat pull downs	4	8,8,8,8
cable crossovers	4	8,8,6,6

Day 2

exercise	sets	reps
incline barbell bench press	5	8,6,4,2,1
barbell military press	5	8,6,4,2,1
seated cable rows	4	8,8,8,8
squats	5	10,8,6,4,2
incline flyes	4	8,6,4,2
lunges	5	10,8,6,4,2
close-grip lat pull downs	4	8,8,8,8
barbell bench press	4	8,8,6,6

Day 3

exercise	sets	reps
barbell bench press	5	8,6,4,2,1
barbell military press	5	8,6,4,2,1
bent-over barbell rows	4	8,8,8,8
leg press	5	10,8,6,4,2
incline barbell bench press	4	8,6,4,2
dead lift	5	10,8,6,4,2
wide-grip lat pull downs	4	8,8,8,8
cable crossovers	4	8,8,6,6

Program Level IV
Strength Training
Two-Day Split 4 days per week
Upper & lower body training on different days

Weeks 1 and 2

Days 1 and 3

exercise	sets	reps
barbell bench press	5	8,6,4,2,1
wide-grip lat pull downs	4	8,8,8,8
barbell military press	5	8,6,4,2,1
hammer curls	4	12,10,8,6
close-grip barbell bench press	4	10,10,8,8
bent-over barbell rows	4	8,8,8,8

Days 2 and 4

exercise	sets	reps
squats	5	10,8,6,4,2
leg press	5	10,8,6,4,2
leg curls	4	8,8,6,6
lunges	4	10,8,8,6
leg extensions	4	8,8,6,6
standing calf raises	4	20,20,20,20

Weeks 3 and 4

Days 1 and 3

exercise	sets	reps
barbell bench press	5	8,6,4,2,1
close-grip lat pull downs	4	8,8,8,8
barbell military press	5	8,6,4,2,1
reverse curls	4	12,10,8,6
incline barbell bench press	4	10,10,8,8
T-bar rows	4	8,8,8,8

Days 2 and 4

exercise	sets	reps
leg press	5	10,8,6,4,2
squats	5	10,8,6,4,2
lunges	4	10,8,6,4,2
leg extensions	4	10,8,8,6
leg curls	4	8,8,6,6
standing calf raises	4	20,20,20,20

Program Level IV
Strength Training
Three-Day Split four days a week -- Antagonistic Training

Weeks 1 and 2

Day 1

exercise	sets	reps
barbell bench press	5	8,6,4,2,1
incline barbell bench press	5	8,6,4,2,1
wide-grip lat pull downs	4	8,8,8,8
seated cable rows	4	8,8,8,8
cable crossovers	4	8,8,6,6
bent-over barbell rows	4	8,8,8,8
incline flyes	4	10,8,6,6
T-bar rows	4	8,8,8,8

Day 2

exercise	sets	reps
squats	5	10,8,6,4,2
leg press	5	10,8,6,4,2
barbell military press	5	8,6,4,2,1
upright rows	4	8,8,6,6
lunges	4	10,8,8,6
barbell shrugs	4	10,8,8,6
dead lift	5	10,8,6,4,2
bent-over lateral raises	4	10,8,8,6

Day 3

exercise	sets	reps
barbell triceps curls	5	12,10,8,6,2
close-grip barbell bench press	5	12,10,8,6,2
hammer curls	4	12,10,8,6
preacher curls	4	12,10,8,6
bench dips	5	12,10,8,6,2
barbell curls	4	12,10,8,6
skull crushers	5	12,10,8,6,2
concentration curls	4	12,10,8,6

Weeks 3 and 4

Day 1

exercise	sets	reps
barbell bench press	5	8,6,4,2,1
incline barbell bench press	5	8,6,4,2,1
close-grip lat pull downs	4	8,8,8,8
T-bar rows	4	8,8,8,8
flyes	4	10,8,8,6
behind the neck pull downs	4	8,8,8,8
cable crossovers	4	10,8,8,6
bent-over barbell rows	4	8,8,8,8

Day 2

exercise	sets	reps
squats	5	10,8,6,4,2
dead lift	5	10,8,6,4,2
barbell military press	5	8,6,4,2,1
standing flyes	4	8,8,6,6
lunges	4	10,8,8,6
barbell shrugs	4	10,8,8,6
leg press	5	10,8,6,4,2
upright rows	4	8,8,6,6

Day 3

exercise	sets	reps
barbell triceps curls	5	12,10,8,6,2
triceps push downs	5	12,10,8,6,2
reverse barbell curls	4	12,10,8,6
barbell curls	4	12,10,8,6
dips	5	12,10,8,6,2
preacher curls	4	12,10,8,6
skull crushers	5	12,10,8,6,2
incline dumbbell curls	4	12,10,8,6

Program Level IV
Strength Training

Three-Day Split four days a week -- Synergistic Training

Weeks 1 and 2

Day 1

exercise	sets	reps
barbell bench press	5	8,6,4,2,1
incline barbell bench press	5	8,6,4,2,1
close-grip barbell bench press	5	8,6,4,2,1
triceps push downs	4	12,10,8,6
flyes	4	10,8,8,6
skull crushers	5	12,10,8,6,2
dips	4	8,8,8,8
barbell triceps curls	5	12,10,8,6,2

Day 2

exercise	sets	reps
wide-grip lat pull downs	4	8,8,8,8
hammer curls	4	12,10,8,6
preacher curls	4	12,10,8,6
bent-over barbell rows	4	8,8,8,8
seated cable rows	4	8,8,8,8
barbell curls	4	12,10,8,6
incline dumbbell curls	4	12,10,8,6
T-bar rows	4	8,8,8,8

Day 3

exercise	sets	reps
squats	5	10,8,6,4,2
leg press	5	10,8,6,4,2
barbell military press	5	8,6,4,2,1
upright rows	4	8,8,6,6
lunges	4	10,8,8,6
standing flyes	4	8,8,6,6
leg extensions	4	8,8,6,6
lateral raises	4	8,8,8,8

Weeks 3 and 4

Day 1

exercise	sets	reps
barbell bench press	5	8,6,4,2,1
incline barbell bench press	5	8,6,4,2,1
dumbbell triceps curls	4	8,6,6,6
triceps pull downs	4	12,10,8,6
incline flyes	4	10,8,8,6
one-arm triceps extensions	5	12,10,8,6,2
bench dips	4	8,8,8,8
triceps kickbacks	4	8,8,8,8

Day 2

exercise	sets	reps
close-grip lat pull downs	4	8,8,8,8
reverse barbell curls	4	12,10,8,6
concentration curls	4	12,10,8,6
behind the neck pull downs	4	8,8,8,8
seated cable rows	4	8,8,8,8
barbell curls	4	12,10,8,6
dumbbell curls	4	12,10,8,6
one-arm dumbbell rows	4	8,8,8,8

Day 3

exercise	sets	reps
squats	5	10,8,6,4,2
dead lift	5	10,8,6,4,2
barbell military press	5	8,6,4,2,1
upright rows	4	8,8,6,6
leg curls	4	10,8,8,6
standing flyes	4	8,8,6,6
standing calf raises	4	20,20,20,20
front raises	4	8,8,8,8

Program Level IV
Strength Training

Two-Day Split 4 days per week -- Upper & lower body training on the same day -- Antagonistic Training

Weeks 1 and 2

Days 1 and 3

exercise	sets	reps
barbell bench press	5	8,6,4,2,1
wide-grip lat pull downs	4	8,8,8,8
incline barbell bench press	5	8,6,4,2,1
barbell military press	5	10,8,6,4,2
leg curls	5	8,6,4,2,1
standing calf raises	4	20,20,20,20

Days 2 and 4

exercise	sets	reps
squats	5	10,8,6,4,2
leg press	5	10,8,6,4,2
barbell curls	4	12,10,8,6
skull crushers	5	12,10,8,6,2
hammer curls	4	12,10,8,6
barbell triceps curls	4	12,10,8,6

Weeks 3 and 4

Days 1 and 3

exercise	sets	reps
barbell bench press	5	8,6,4,2,1
close-grip lat pull downs	4	8,8,8,8
barbell military press	5	8,6,4,2,1
leg curls	5	10,8,6,4,2
good mornings	4	15,15,15,15
incline barbell bench press	5	8,6,4,2,1

Days 2 and 4

exercise	sets	reps
squats	5	10,8,6,4,2
dead lift	5	10,8,6,4,2
preacher curls	4	12,10,8,6
triceps push downs	4	12,10,8,6
reverse curls	4	12,10,8,6
triceps kickbacks	4	12,10,8,6

Program Level IV
Strength Training
Two-Day Split 4 days per week

Upper & lower body training on the same day
Synergistic Training

Weeks 1 and 2

Days 1 and 3

exercise	sets	reps
barbell bench press	5	8,6,4,2,1
barbell military press	5	8,6,4,2,1
incline barbell bench press	5	8,6,4,2,1
leg curls	5	10,8,6,4,2
close grip barbell bench press	4	10,10,8,8
good mornings	4	15,15,15,15

Days 2 and 4

exercise	sets	reps
wide-grip lat pull downs	4	8,8,8,8
hammer curls	4	12,10,8,6
squats	5	10,8,6,4,2
leg extensions	4	8,8,6,6
bent-over rows	4	8,8,8,8
lunges	4	10,8,8,6

Weeks 3 and 4

Days 1 and 3

exercise	sets	reps
barbell bench press	5	8,6,4,2,1
barbell military press	5	8,6,4,2,1
incline barbell bench press	5	8,6,4,2,1
leg curls	5	10,8,6,4,2
barbell triceps curls	4	10,10,8,8
standing calf raises	4	20,20,20,20

Days 2 and 4

exercise	sets	reps
close-grip lat pull downs	4	8,8,8,8
reverse curls	4	12,10,8,6
leg press	5	10,8,6,4,2
leg extensions	4	8,8,6,6
bent-over barbell rows	4	8,8,8,8
dead lift	5	10,8,6,4,2

Program Level V
Strength Training
Two-Day Split 4 days per week

Upper & lower body training on the same day
Antagonistic Training

Weeks 1 and 2

Days 1 and 3

exercise	sets	reps
barbell bench press	5	8,6,4,2,1
wide-grip lat pull downs	4	8,8,8,8
barbell military press	5	8,6,4,2,1
leg curls	5	10,8,6,4,2
incline barbell bench press	5	8,6,4,2,1
standing calf raises	4	20,20,20,20
T-bar rows	4	8,8,8,8
standing flyes	4	8,8,6,6

Days 2 and 4

exercise	sets	reps
squats	5	10,8,6,4,2
leg press	5	10,8,6,4,2
barbell curls	4	12,10,8,6
skull crushers	5	12,10,8,6,2
hammer curls	4	12,10,8,6
barbell triceps curls	4	12,10,8,6
lunges	4	10,8,8,6
triceps push downs	4	12,10,8,6

Weeks 3 and 4

Days 1 and 3

exercise	sets	reps
barbell bench press	5	8,6,4,2,1
close-grip lat pull downs	4	8,8,8,8
barbell military press	5	8,6,4,2,1
leg curls	5	10,8,6,4,2
good mornings	4	15,15,15,15
incline barbell bench press	5	8,6,4,2,1
seated cable rows	4	8,8,8,8
upright rows	4	8,8,6,6

Days 2 and 4

exercise	sets	reps
squats	5	10,8,6,4,2
dead lift	5	10,8,6,4,2
preacher curls	4	12,10,8,6
triceps push downs	4	12,10,8,6
reverse curls	4	12,10,8,6
barbell triceps curls	4	12,10,8,6
standing calf raises	4	20,20,20,20
bench dips	3	15,15,15

Program Level V
Strength Training
Two-Day Split 4 days per week
Upper & lower body training on different days

Weeks 1 and 2

Days 1 and 3

exercise	sets	reps
barbell bench press	5	8,6,4,2,1
wide-grip lat pull downs	4	8,8,8,8
barbell military press	5	8,6,4,2,1
hammer curls	4	12,10,8,6
close-grip barbell bench press	4	10,10,8,8
bent-over barbell rows	4	8,8,8,8
incline barbell bench press	5	8,6,4,2,1
skull crushers	5	12,10,8,6,2

Days 2 and 4

exercise	sets	reps
squats	5	10,8,6,4,2
leg press	5	10,8,6,4,2
standing calf raises	4	20,20,20,20
lunges	4	10,8,8,6
leg extensions	4	8,8,6,6
leg curls	4	8,8,6,6
dead lift	4	8,6,4,2
seated calf raises	4	20,20,20,20

Weeks 3 and 4

Days 1 and 3

exercise	sets	reps
barbell bench press	5	8,6,4,2,1
close-grip lat pull downs	4	8,8,8,8
barbell military press	5	8,6,4,2,1
reverse curls	4	12,10,8,6
incline barbell bench press	4	10,10,8,8
T-bar rows	4	8,8,8,8
barbell triceps curls	5	12,10,8,6,2
barbell curls	5	12,10,8,6,2

Days 2 and 4

exercise	sets	reps
leg press	5	10,8,6,4,2
squats	5	10,8,6,4,2
lunges	4	10,8,6,4,2
dead lift	4	10,8,8,6
leg curls	4	8,8,6,6
leg extensions	4	8,8,6,6
standing calf raises	4	8,6,4,2
seated calf raises	4	20,20,20,20

Program Level V
Strength Training

Two-Day Split 4 days per week
Upper & lower body training on the same day
Synergistic Training

Weeks 1 and 2

Days 1 and 3

exercise	sets	reps
barbell bench press	5	8,6,4,2,1
barbell military press	5	8,6,4,2,1
incline barbell bench press	5	8,6,4,2,1
leg curls	5	10,8,6,4,2
close-grip barbell bench press	4	10,10,8,8
good mornings	4	15,15,15,15
skull crushers	5	12,10,8,6,2
upright rows	4	8,8,6,6

Days 2 and 4

exercise	sets	reps
wide-grip lat pull downs	4	8,8,8,8
hammer curls	4	12,10,8,6
squats	5	10,8,6,4,2
leg extensions	4	8,8,6,6
bent-over barbell rows	4	8,8,8,8
lunges	4	10,8,8,6
T-bar rows	4	8,8,8,8
preacher curls	4	12,10,8,6

Weeks 3 and 4

Days 1 and 3

exercise	sets	reps
barbell bench press	5	8,6,4,2,1
barbell military press	5	8,6,4,2,1
incline barbell bench press	5	8,6,4,2,1
leg curls	5	10,8,6,4,2
barbell triceps curls	4	10,10,8,8
standing calf raises	4	20,20,20,20
triceps pull downs	4	12,10,8,6
standing flyes	4	8,8,6,6

Days 2 and 4

exercise	sets	reps
close-grip lat pull downs	4	8,8,8,8
reverse curls	4	12,10,8,6
leg press	5	10,8,6,4,2
leg extensions	4	8,8,6,6
bent-over barbell rows	4	8,8,8,8
dead lift	5	10,8,6,4,2
seated cable rows	4	8,8,8,8
barbell curls	4	12,10,8,6

Notes

the SportsBuddy

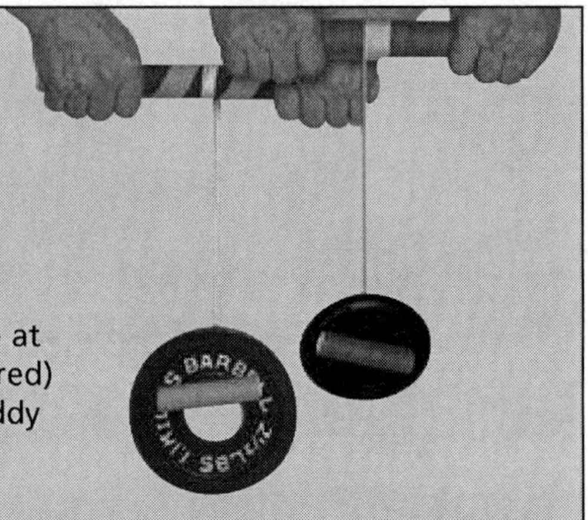

To prepare the Sports Buddy, place the small piece at the bottom of the string through a plate (as pictured) so that you are able to securely use the Sports Buddy to lift the plate off the ground.

Starting Position

Hold the Sports Buddy out in front of your body with your arms extended and your hands at both ends using an overhand grip. For maximum results, grip the Sports Buddy with your index fingers and thumbs in the air not touching the Sports Buddy.

General Instructions

1. Slowly roll your wrists and hands backwards winding the weight up to the roller.
2. At this point, slowly lower the weight back to its original position by rolling your wrists and hands forward.
3. Next, continue with the same motion of rolling your wrists forward slowly, bringing the weight back up to the roller.
4. Finally, slowly lower the weight back to its original position by rolling your wrists and hands backwards and repeat.

If your main goal is to increase the strength in your dominant forearm and wrist, then wind the string to the same side as the arm you are trying to work. This will make the arm work harder when using the Sports Buddy.

Recommended weight to use with the Sports Buddy: 2.5 lbs

If you don t want to travel to the gym every day to use the Sports Buddy, you can purchase weights at ANY sporting goods store for about $1.00 to $2.00 each.

***sports*workout.com**

Notes